The
Woodmill Farm
Blog Book

by Michelle Hume

AuthorHouse™ UK Ltd.
500 Avebury Boulevard
Central Milton Keynes, MK9 2BE
www.authorhouse.co.uk
Phone: 08001974150

First published by AuthorHouse 11/12/2008

ISBN: 978-1-4343-9798-0 (sc)

This book is printed on acid-free paper.

Printed in the United States of America
Bloomington, Indiana

Monday, 21 May 2007

Before Woodmill

Well, I thought I would write a very ill-prepared grammatical nightmare blog! It all began when we went on holiday to Finland in August 2006. Such a beautiful country; a log cabin with our own boat and animals at our finger tips and the pressure of work left behind. Needless to say, upon our return the itchy feet syndrome appeared! Laura and I thought that getting a new pet would help, so set about finding a tortoise. After many discussions, to put it mildly, the decision was made to postpone the tortoise until we lived in an appropriate house with large gardens or land. The house went on the market the very next day — we don't hang around! It was a brave decision in retrospect, as Steven lived walking distance to both schools, the one he is attending and the one he will be attending, and had a good friend living nearby. Laura was also in this position. Although itchy feet sparked us into action, it wasn't because we disliked the house we were in, it was a beautiful house, we had only just finished renovation and I must say I loved it; the outlook on the pond, the way the house flowed; and our neighbours were great too! But Pete had handed in his notice at work after 18 years, and was a director at the time, to set up on our own. Us being us thought that time for a change was nigh, and went the whole 9 yards, putting it mildly. I closed my interior company, Pete left his job, we sold up and moved to pastures new; financially crippled, but hey, life is for living and we were about to do a whole load of that — but not in the way we used to do it!

Tuesday, 22 May 2007

First few memories of Woodmill Farm

Well, what can I say? We moved to Woodmill on the 16th January 2007. Inherited hens, guinea pigs and a pig. No idea what to do with any of them, a steep learning curve was ahead. Luckily, Caroline and John, who we bought Woodmill from, were around to give a helping hand and advice, and boy did we need it. So very grateful to them! We set about spring cleaning the cottages; they were, and are, beautiful. I would be most impressed if I came to holiday in them! The weather was grotty for a number of weeks, and the rain just didn't stop. The bottom paddock was flooded, due to a natural spring, by the pigs, and we were up to our knees in mud and water, and that's just the animals. We had to sort a hosting company out, a web designer, and organise brochures and letterheads. Luckily for us, Paul Bradforth and Annie Webster, who we had worked with before on our Purl Design website, were to hand. Extremely talented people, and they were on site taking photos the day we moved in and, hey presto: letterheads and business cards were on the way (I am sure it wasn't that easy!). The cottage we lived in needed renovating, and it became apparent very quickly a re-wire was on the cards! Our other company, which deals in sustainable architecture, needed to take the pressure financially until we had guests coming in, and being a new company we didn't know if this was going to happen. Pete is very well thought of in the world of architecture (he is very modest, so I have to sing his praises!) and the work soon came in; probably more than we could deal with, but there are 24 hours in a day, and we worked all of them!

Just as we thought life couldn't get any more hectic

Well Laura's birthday soon was upon us, and in all our madness we needed to make her 16th special for her. She had always wanted a pony so off I went in search of one! Caroline came with me, as she knew far more than I did about such animals! Blisland was the place, a field full of miniature Shetlands were in front of us and David the farmer said have a look and see what you like; well, how could you choose? Such pretty little things, I would have had them all. We saw one, and it seemed a baby one was following her around; I mentioned perhaps we should take a closer look and, with that, David started to drive them to separate them! They all just bolted and went everywhere; me and Caroline, no better than each other, just couldn't stop laughing: what a fiasco! Finally got the two we wanted, and they were in the van and on the way home before we knew it! I had a fleeting moment of reality and thought I had better tell Pete! I telephoned and said I was on the way home with a couple of friends! Turned up with the ponies; another very steep learning curve. We released them into our field, and just let them settle in until Laura came back from school. She was absolutely delighted; her face was a picture. Two scruffy little ponies; one probably was in foal, but not sure, and the other just a baby, both with winter coats and extremely messy; but she loved them.

And then it was Steven's birthday

I suppose it doesn't matter how many animals you have. Steven really wanted a puppy and we thought, well if we can't do it now, when can we do it? We already had a rescue dog called Gem who was a complete hairball, but lovely with it, cross between a monkey and a badger I guess! And then along came Lucky, a Sprocker; boy was she a lively and still is, a complete nightmare, but so adorable; you just couldn't be cross ...

And then there were pigs

We had to get to grips with the pig situation! We went to see David from Walter Baileys; he was the one that knew everything there was to know about pigs! He decided not to breed for a while, and we bought his breeding stock, and named them Rosie, Daisy and Oscar! I am not sure whether David would have rubbed their bellies, but they are so cute; if you rub their bellies, they just fall over and let you do it, they are so funny. And they know their names, they come when they are called. I am not sure I would make a farmer, but it's not good to all be the same in life! David has been so good to us, as have Steve and Adam; mind you I think my clients should just pay them direct the amount it costs us every month ...

Wednesday 23 May 2007
Ducks!

I heard a noise from the rushes, it was the most strange loud noise. I went to the pond to investigate and there beneath my feet was the smallest duckling I have ever seen. He ran from the rushes straight over to me. I hadn't realised the mum was sitting; I picked him up and after no sign of the mum, I thought I had better get him warm, so tried to get Henrietta to sit on him, but she wasn't having any of it! I eventually found mum, and snuggled the duckling under her, and for the rest of the day, he was a happy duck! They fed in the evening, and were well hidden from everything, with an electric fence. Watch this space!

Our new arrival on 20 April

I am trying to bring you all up to date, but I am fast realising that so much has happened, and happens on a daily basis, that this is impossible, so if I jump around a bit on remembering things, please excuse me. I will just post what I remember on any given day, and just try to update you regularly!

Oh, just remembered: haven't told you about the foal!

Marble, Laura's pony, was, in fact, pregnant, and the proof of the pudding lay before us on the 20th April 2007. Laura went down to feed as usual and after waiting for weeks thinking Marble was going to have a foal — "was she/wasn't she?" thing going on — it was a bit of a surprise, as we and our guests had given up, really!

The tiniest body lay in the corner with his mum looking on. I had a phone call from Laura's mobile to come quick; Tommaso was born, Marble was a proud mum of a little boy; so were we! Tommaso was so called after a little boy who came to stay with us a few weeks before and was the cutest child I have ever seen; Nadia, his mum, and Alistair, his Dad — lovely people. I hope we will see them again; I am not very good at Italian, even a small child was better than I!

We called at all the cottages and got them out of bed to see our new addition, it was so exciting!

We rang everyone about his birth; all the guests who had stayed before, especially Shirley who had kept a vigil whilst staying here, and friends and family were all told …

Finally got the children to school and returned to see if Tommaso had taken his first feed — and that's where the problems began!

Tomasso our little battler

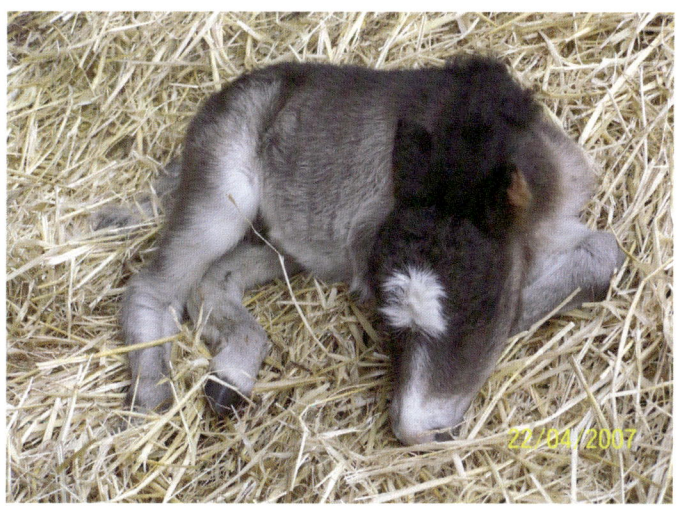

It is difficult to backtrack, but Tom was so poorly he didn't have his first feed, and the vet was called. He came, and said it's just a slim chance Tom will make it; we proceeded to do what needed to be done (I say we, but I mean the vet; Pete and I sort of helped, if you can call it that!). We did what we could to assist the vet. Marble, a wild pony, not head collared, needed to be milked to try to save this foal. What a game that was; I won't bore you with the details, but we then had to tube this milk to Tom's belly. After several visits, Tom was getting worse, and was finally moved to animal hospital with his mum. It was found he was not able to suckle; after a long haul, the vets (Ben, Pete, Nikki and everyone else had a huge hand in him living at all) got him on a bottle and he was back home, far from out of the woods, it went from bad to worse, with Tom contracting infections, fungal and others. But he battled through, and sometimes we just lay with him in the hay, so he would feel a heart beat; every hour we were feeding at some points. His mum, not able to feed him, rejected him; not in a bad way, just not getting close to him ...

So it was up to us. We gave up every hour to try to make him live, and it was hard; but not as hard as losing him would have been ...

Probiotics, goat's milk, goat's yoghurts, foal feed ... advice from Becs down at Baileys! She knows all there is to know about horses, and a huge help. Visits to the vets, in the car, and sat with the dogs and cats, as he was only 10 kg. He became a real attraction. He never was expected to live and after 4 weeks he is still here; not without problems, but we are trying to get through them one at a time. I wish I started the blog then, as there was so much that went on; still, go from here ...

Feeding Tom

Well today: feeding time. Tom fed well today; I had to buy some horse shampoo to wash his backside! He has the runs at the moment! Another little set back, hoping the probiotics will help this. Sorted out a bucket of bubbles; the postman came and I had to briefly sign for a letter and, with that, Tom put his whole head — and I mean his whole head — in the bucket of bubbles; he looked like a snow man! He's out in the paddock with Duke, our 20 year old gelding, and Marble, his mum, trying to be a horse! Feed time at 1pm again.

The Buzzards came

Some really sad news I am afraid: our tiny duckling and mum were both attacked on the edge of the rushes by a buzzard; we lost them both.

I was so upset; our first fatality. I know nature must take its course, but it's hard sometimes to think like that. Maybe if she ever hatches another egg and we find the duckling, we could remove her and hand rear …

It is not often they hatch as there are so many predators.

Happier news — we have Chicks

Well who'd have thought it: chicks … from eggs! Only kidding; but I must say I was surprised to see six yellow fluffy things emerge from the eggs. They eat like hunters; I seem to be constantly feeding them at the moment; perhaps they are crossed with ostriches! Henrietta, our Red hen, has hatched just one. She wanted to sit, and we let her only one egg but it made her happy! And she is now the proud mum of one; I think we have to keep them separated for 8 weeks from the rest of the tribe and then introduce them; have to seek advice on that. Oh, Walter Bailey's again I guess!

Thursday 24 May 2007

I have come a long way — chickens do not need umbrellas!

Just thinking back to funny moments, this springs to mind (bearing in mind I have only ever had a garden and residential animals: this is my excuse and I am sticking to it!) The chickens weren't feeding too good and I was worried the egg supply would dry up; I figured out that they didn't like the food when it got wet. So I decided in my wisdom that, when feeding time came around, I would shelter them whilst they ate, thus getting my eggs, and them fed. I stood there in the pouring rain with my umbrella, shielding these feathered friends from the rain — not just on one occasion either! I made the mistake of telling Adam from Baileys, and he nearly fell to the floor laughing. So I guess I learned: chickens don't need umbrellas!

Cowboy ... I think not!

Well Pete was in his element making a fence and rounding up the horses ... he's always wanted to be a cowboy! Well, I think he got carried away with his duffer (technical term for post whacker-inner) He was going great guns and the posts were going in real quick. Then the thuds stopped! He had knocked himself out; the duffer had sprung up and landed on his head, and Pete was there on the floor with stars about his head! After I had stopped laughing, I thought I'd better see if he was ok ... he was fine. Just looked like the morning after the night before, if you get my drift! Think he's going to have to work at that Cowboy thing!

Thought I'd let the pigs out!

Well, today was sunny and the pigs had a bad start; Daisy did anyway; she had to be ringed today. So I thought I would cheer them up and let them in Steven's footy area; they had a ball, pardon the pun! We sat and had a chat, played in the Buttercups and had an hour or so of time with them ... then I realised I hadn't turned the cottage around and it was 2.30 and I was expecting new guests at 4! All hands on deck ... pigs away, Pete to shop, me to laundry ... vacuum, polish and broom in hand! Finish quick smart, visitors came whilst I was feeding Tom, Duke the gelding got out and was on the "grass is greener" phase ... got Pete (a guest) to keep an eye on Duke whilst thrusting a feed bottle in his hand for Tom, and trying to appear like all was under control ... thought I had just pulled it off, when I realised I had left the scones in the oven for their arrival ... aaahhh ... was just caught in the nick of time — scones intact!

The toy arrived

24/05/2007

After waiting forever for a ride-on Lawn mower, it was here. No more trying to make the animals eat it, so Steven can play football in his paddock! The lawn mower had arrived ... always wanted one! Sad but true! No more disputes over who is cutting the grass eh!

Teaching Tom to be a horse!

Tom, being hand reared, was in danger of being a nightmare apparently, if he didn't learn how to be a horse, according to the Vets! So initially I tried him with the other ponies but he was too fragile. I thought the only way to do it is if I act as his mum and teach him! And boy am I glad there are no photos available ... I was on all fours in the paddock teaching him that he must eat grass ... picking bits and putting them in his mouth ... this can't be right ... but desperate measures were necessary if he was going to survive and be able to be in the paddock with the other ponies! Otherwise he was going to be a house pony. He had already made himself at home in front of the fire, conservatory and kitchen! I think it worked anyway, as Tom is now with his mum Marble and Duke, quite comfortable, and is mimicking eating grass but is unable to at the moment, as he only has bottom teeth and no top ones as yet!

The Drake was saved!

It was a cold wet evening when the geese and ducks kicked off. We raced out to see what all the commotion was about, only to find the goose and gander were drowning the drake ... Bernie our Drake. I couldn't believe it ... dived in to get the drake out ... he was motionless and cold ... still had a heart beat, so there was hope. We wrapped him up and put him in front the rayburn, in a cat box! We rubbed his chest to get the water out from inside him. Not sure if he was going to make it; we (well that might have been me!) decided to keep him in that night. I just couldn't rest; I moved him by the bed and kept an eye on him all night. In the morning he was still there; a little better, but very poorly. Off to the vets (yes, I know you can buy drakes for two quid each, but this was Bernie our Drake we are talking about, not some old duck!) £40 later they couldn't find the problem ... he just kept losing his balance. Turned the stable into a duck hospital, and after 5 days of constant care and rehabilitation, he was ready to release back to his mate, Bruno! We saved him! Needless to say the geese were relocated that night!

Saturday 26 May 2007

Now that's what I call a Fairy Godmother!

Always glad to see family! Especially when they arrive with wellies and a rake in hand! My Aunt Louise, alias my godmother, arrived from Spain to see the new pad! Luckily for me she was up for a bit of hard work; after a week of nettle clearing and horse mucking out, I think she was ready for a cup of tea! Doug helped too, he even cut the grass, poor guy! I treated her real well ... even gave her an evening meal ... chips! No sausage, as we ran out of money, and even the bread (for chip butty!) had just been fed to the ducks, and 2 pickles between us! Ah we know how to live!

Any ideas from those who know about ponies?

Tom still not feeding real well ... he is on probiotics and is still on made-up foal milk, but he still has the runs! He seems to be well in himself, and the results from the vets are OK ... but his tummy is still poorly. Any handy hints to try would be much appreciated. He is still a 24-7 job, but we love him!

Not sure I should be let loose!

Bought a petrol hedge trimmer; thought this would be good, real quick to tidy up. I was away, chopping everything I could see! Alan Titchmarsh, eat your heart out! I stood back and looked at my work: um very nice, do more tomorrow—until I went in! No cooker, no sockets. no power anywhere. Thought I must have had a power cut, until I looked up and saw Pete pointing to the remains of what used to be our electric cable; I had gone right through it! Usually there would have been sparks, or me on the floor; nothing of significance happened, our electrician couldn't believe it when he came: 1, that I was still standing and 2, that I had been so stupid! Ah that Alan Harris is a good man! He fixed it in no time (when he got back from that Steve Andrews place!)

Sunday 27 May 2007

Studley, our stallion ... too much to handle!

There are many stories about Studley our stallion, this being one that springs to mind now. I didn't name him by the way. Liz and Pip (our guests) will remember this well. It was 6am and the most awful noise was coming from

outside, Pete thought it was cats fighting, but it was definitely worse than that. I looked out the window and Studley had broken through the hedge and was fighting with Duke our gelding. I ran to the door; meanwhile Liz came to the door to raise the alarm. In a flash we were all just up and out of bed and trying to part these males; all the horses were going mad. Managed to part Duke and take him out of the field — he is 20 and his heart just isn't up to that. With that, Studley ran and chased Tilly. Liz was one end and Pip the other, trying to close the field off, just so we could get Studley in the field on his own. After a frantic hour, we all managed. Studley was tied up and returned to his paddock. We just couldn't risk this again. Pete was out at 7am making all the hedges and fences higher; you don't expect to be in the field in your PJs on your holiday do you? We were extremely grateful for their help; I think they enjoyed it really — a world away from their usual life!

Adios! Thank youX

Well, it was time for Louise and Doug to return to the heat of sunny Spain. They had a few bricks to chew along the way and then off to build their wall. They were paid in tea and chips! We are hoping they may return to Woodmill for a little more hard labour; may have to review the pay structure and include a sausage!

Time out!

As we now live in the historic valley of Luxuylan, we thought we would take an hour off in our hectic life (and this is the first hour since the 16th January!) to walk the valley. What a beautiful place, so peaceful and tranquil; the water just meanders down through the mossy boulders — love it! We have a puppy Springer, Lucky, who hasn't had

the chance to go swimming before, so Pete in his wisdom decides that today is the day — Gem goes in first then Lucky; Gem already knows the ropes and finds a safe area in which to swim. Lucky however, is a different kettle of fish! Goes straight out to the faster flowing part and was getting carried away down stream. Ok so the water wasn't going really fast, but enough to worry us. Pete jumped to a boulder to catch her and fell in himself! Finally all were on dry land; we returned home, Lucky and Pete like two soggy squelching sponges; imagine what we would be like with two hours to spare!

Just a regular day!

What a day and it's not even lunch time yet. Tom not feeding too good, Lucky got out — someone who shall remain nameless left the gate open (Martin!), one of the ducks went AWOL, the pigs got out — forgot to turn on the electric fence! Whilst chasing the duck, it rains; ran to get Tom in — ducks gone further. Pigs now chasing ponies — Storm, our rug rat of a pony, was racing around like a looney. Manged to get pigs in, Steven needs to go to a golf competition, Laura needs to be in town for something, Tom's feed is here again. Got ducks in, covered in mud. Deliver kids, feed foal, and its only 12.20!

Monday 28 May 2007

Our famous, or should that be infamous, guests!

What a crew! Extremely talented musicians were out singing on the veranda, free entertainment! Great! A lovely summer's evening, what a treat! I think they owed it to me after what they did to me the night before ... Jackie heard a bell noise coming from the boiler the night before and asked me to investigate. After trying to sort the boiler for a while, I was kindly let in on the joke — a receiver had been put on top of the boiler and the bell in someones pocket! so every time I looked for the problem, the bell went off! Ah the week is young; I will have to think of something! I won't mention his name but the main culprit is the one in the middle of this picture (yes you know who you are!)

Tuesday 29 May 2007

Tom's first taste of grass

Tommaso had his first real taste of grass today — what a huge step forward. Until now, he has mimicked eating grass but not actually chewed or swallowed it! Today he managed it; only a little, but he did it. Let's hope it goes from strength to strength. He also had his first indoor bath! Extremely smelly; it was too big a job for the bucket and sponge, a bath was necessary. I brought him in, filled the bath with bubbles, and gave him a good clean. I think it gave him a bit of energy! He was off running around the field in no time.

Wednesday 30 May 2007

Woodmill United!

Martin, Pete's brother and accomplished poet (his books are available to read or purchase in the cottages) came to stay with us. A football team was in the making. Gem, Tom and Martin ... any ideas for a right back and goalie?

Jackie and Sue with Tom

I think our guests Jackie and Sue had taken a real shine to Tom, they were his surrogate aunties! And he was lapping up the attention! Lovely people, hope they come and stay with us again. Jackie loves animals and I think if she could get away with it, would take Tom home! Sue had reared blackbirds and young sparrows, which I would love to do — hopefully at some point I will get that opportunity. Sue has had a lot of pets in the past and has many handy hints! They fed Tom yesterday, quite successfully — thanks Auntie Sue and Auntie Jackie!

BBQ for the famous!

No more practical jokes — well not yet anyway. Our famous musicians have switched from strumming to cooking! Beautiful weather at the moment, ideal for a BBQ or two! Mind you theirs was a little more successful than ours; ours had an air of blackness about it, whilst theirs looked good enough to eat!

Dogs — who'd have 'em!

What a day! Lucky, our little angel of a springer puppy (I think not!) was a little too lively for our 20 month old great nephew (that makes us sound like 105!), so we separated them. She spent an hour or two out the back porch area. I thought she was quiet; I opened the door and saw why she had been so quiet — all of the toilet roll from the downstairs loo had been strewn around the floor, the mat had been chewed, Steven's school bag emptied! What an absolute mess; she just sat there in all this and looked at me as if to say: "Wasn't me, I didn't do it, no-one saw me; you can't prove anything!"

A companion for Milky the Guinea Pig

Milky hasn't quite been the same since she lost her daughter Fudge, so we thought it was high time we did something about it! Pete thought Steven and I were collecting some photos of Laura's ball, but we came back with a rabbit, a seven week old lop eared rabbit ... Milky was going to love her! Brought her home, thought I would leave her in the box for a minute or so and then introduce her to Milky, but within seconds she leaped out of the box across the kitchen and was off! Luckily, Lucky didn't catch her! Perhaps it was best if she got introduced to Milky now! They both seem fine — hopefully a friendship is on the horizon ...

Saturday 2 June 2007

Yippee, our Website is live!

Well after working hard on the website, it finally (I say finally, but it didn't take long really) went live, and we had two on line bookings ... how great was that for the first day? Paul Bradforth was the brains behind it — I just gave him the information he asked for, and he made it look wonderful! So guys, if you ever need anything, Paul is the man! Great photographer; he did all the inside shots, plus the front page, and fantastic web designer! See, all in one neat package!

My famous guys went home!

Well, Saturday came quickly this week and our famous musicians went home, along with Auntie Sue, Jackie and Jayne. Tom will miss them! We had a lovely week with them, shame the weather wasn't great every day, we could have had music every night! I am sure I will be hearing from them shortly, with a few photos — there is a special one I need to post on this blog, and when it comes, you'll know why — I couldn't believe my eyes! Great to meet you all, hope you all come back. And if you ever get the chance to hear Paul Williams, then do so: well worth listening to, an extremely talented guitarist.

Butter wouldn't melt!

You look at this beautiful puppy and think ahhhh, how cute; how sweet. Well that's what Pete's brother Martin though, until he had a shower. He placed his clothes as far away from the shower as possible, so they didn't get wet, and as we are still renovating, (listen to me — we have only been here five minutes!) we haven't got any hooks on the door yet. So the clothes were on the floor by the door; Martin saw them start to disappear from beneath the door — he jumped out of the baby Betty bath/shower thing, and this is difficult if you know what this is; went flying through the downstairs bathroom to have a tug of war with his clothes — *Mmmm, cute puppy — I think not!*

OK, I give in!

Ok, ok so I give up: I have Pete wanting to be like a cowboy; fences, horses and the like — now Laura has caught the bug, only she dressed like one! I hope this is a joke, or we're in big trouble — they've all gone mad! Good job I'm sane! (now that's a worry: if I'm the normal one ...)

The milk pellets are working, I think

Well, Tom has got past the runny tummy phase ... well for now anyway, which is a huge relief; he was really worrying us. It seemed like a combination between the probiotics and natural yoghurt that helped. He is still feeding 7,10,1,4,7,9,11 and 3am, but we have introduced milk pellets. He is not too sure of them, but today he ate a full measure (50g). So if possible, we are looking to finish the 3am feed and replace with pellets. We will have to see how it goes, I guess. He seems more perky in himself, he was running around like crazy for a while today and tried to buck when I went to wash his backside — I'll try that tomorrow! I feel we are getting somewhere now with him; he's 6 weeks and 1 day.

Sunday 3 June 2007

We've got real problems!

There was a little patch of damp on the ceiling in the lounge. Well, it is a 400 year old cottage; you've got to expect these things. If I were one of my clients, I would have told them to get it investigated, but no, it was us; it could wait — didn't have time — kept forgetting. Well, I was on the phone when it started to pour down with rain, so I shut the door so I could hear better, only to find the rain was, in fact, the water from the upstairs shower pouring through the ceiling in the lounge ...arrghh! All hands on deck; stopped shower, pulled Steven out, got towels — finally stopped the leak. The whole shower and floor had to be pulled out, and the floor will have to be replaced. We don't think it is wet or dry rot, just a long term leak. The ceiling in the shower room came down too, but Pete fixed that with duck tape! I know: only an architect would do this! But hey presto, we have a shower room with no floor or ceiling and a loo in mid air — not bad for a mellow kind of Sunday!

Pete needs glasses!

Either Pete needs glasses or he has finally flipped! I caught him trying to unscrew a knot in the wood on the floor boards! How crazy is that? There was a long line of screws and then the knot, and he thought the knot was another screw!

Beautiful butterfly nearly got the chop!

Today, Pete was merrily strimming away by the chickens and found this beautiful butterfly. If anyone knows what it is can you let us know? I have never seen one before with such vibrant markings — got the butterfly safe. Got no flowers or pretty things left, but hey, they'll grow again — I hope!

Recognise these feet?

If you recognise these feet, beware: they belong to a man that is not safe to strim. He's had the lot today: camellias, fir trees, apple trees and the pretty weeds that I was keeping — *do not let him strim near you!*

Monday 4 June 2007

Toby Toad is here!

Toby and his friends arrived at Woodmill today. They hope they will have a croaking time and will hop up to Eden when they get a minute. Toby said Woodmill was leaps ahead of the other places he had stayed!

Couldn't believe our eyes!

I know we were only used to a regular house and not all the countryside antics, but when I heard a scream from Laura upstairs, I thought she had passed out or something. I didn't expect to see what I saw! Laura, in her final GCSE year, was busy revising. Sky, one of our cats, has a habit of bringing us 'presents', but Laura didn't see her come in with anything. Laura went in her bag to get another revision guide out, and a rabbit jumped out of her school bag — by the time I got up there, it had disappeared again! I thought she was joking — took Sky out, so if there was a rabbit, Sky wouldn't do any more damage than she may have already done. Sure enough, I opened the wardrobe, and the cutest baby rabbit jumped out! A bit of a shock, but how cute — it's not the sort of thing that happens in everyone's bedroom is it? He was released back to the the rest of his family down by the pigs!

Woodmill goes Digital!

We don't actually watch TV, but I know a great many people do, especially in the winter months here. So just over that hill in the photo is where it all comes from, allegedly! It comes from beyond; we are digi-boxed out

here! The signal isn't the strongest I have ever seen, but we are up and running — Digital is here! Anyone would think we just emerged from a cave and seen a cooker for the first time — not far off, I guess!

Tom and Marble had their first intimate moment!

Tom, 6 weeks and 3 days, finally got some close attention from his mum, Marble. I tried to catch it on camera but I was too far away and as I moved closer, they stopped. Marble was lying on the ground and Tom went up and

licked her nose, she reciprocated; wonderful to see, such a privilege to see her connect to Tom for the first time. I hope this is the first of many ... we'll see. Tom is in the shelter now for the night, due a feed at 9pm and 11.30pm, then milk pellets through the night with Probiotic. Feed again at 6.30am (the feeds are foal replacement milk, a bit like SMA for kids), which is when he will rejoin his mum. They used to sleep together; well I say together; they were in the same shelter, and that's about it! But Tom needs to be fed with his feed and I need to know that he has eaten it.

Wednesday 6 June 2007

The chicks are growing!

Aren't chicks cute when they are just born? — all yellow and fluffy. Then they grow! Ours are about 4 weeks now, and still with their mum. We have relocated them down to the chicken pen but still in their run, so they are safe from buzzards and the like, and shut them in at night. They are just starting to get like little thugs! They are always hun-

gry and run over each other to get to the food — they even have little Mohawks coming! Still not sure how to tell boy from girl, but I guess as they grow this will become more apparent!

04/06/2007

Thursday 7 June 2007

Would you trust this pig?

I think the sun has got to the pigs! I thought I would let the pigs out; lovely day — they deserved a long run amongst the trees and flowers, to give the mud pit a break! Well they had just been fed, so I thought all would be well. They

came out of the gate, all chilled and relaxed. So I picked up the bucket; shouldn't have done that, even though it was empty, and tried to walk back up to our cottage. Well, they were like mad things; they chased me and nudged my legs — I nearly went flying; people have had their arms taken off by pigs — this sprung to mind very quickly! I threw the bucket, with chicken feed saucepan and Tom's milk bottle in it, just so I could escape! Rosie was running around with the saucepan in her mouth, Daisy the milk bottle, and Oscar the bucket on his snout! But I was out of there — all I had to do now was figure out how I got all my stuff back! Eventually they followed up the path towards the chickens, eating as they went. All was well, or so I thought! But then they had me surrounded in the chicken pen; I grabbed the pitch fork and prodded them to turn around (only with the blunt end — don't panic!) Finally they realised I was back in charge, and they started to behave!

Woodmill weather station goes live!

Thought it was about time we had the facility to advise our guests of the weather here at Woodmill Farm. A nifty little contraption, should solve all confusion!

I have been here all day!

Yep, Sassy looks an angel. She looks like she has been there all day, not moved a muscle, no, not a paw! Ten minutes before this was taken, I rescued a rabbit (as if we haven't enough of them!) from the jaws of doom. She flew from the floor with a rabbit as big as her, to the top of our porch, through the bedroom window, down the stairs — by

this time we were chasing her — under the stairs, in the bath, and finally caught her on the front lawn, to release a very frightened but unharmed rabbit; just what you need, really!

Just stop for a while

Sometimes in a hectic life, you need to just stop for a while, just for a moment; it needs not much more, to see how beautiful things around you are. I was walking, doing the mundane task of pony poo, when I just stopped to glance at the ducks. The evening sun was bouncing of the still waters of the pond, and the ducks were just quietly duck-diving for grubs. A few splashes of the feet was all you could hear, and a fluffy white bottom is all you could see. Just perfect, so peaceful — they looked so happy.

Friday 8 June 2007

Tom still doing well

Tom and his mum Marble are still getting along, and day by day, there is a little interaction. I don't think they will ever be really close, but she does sort of look for him. He tends to stay close to Duke and Marble whilst grazing

(he isn't actually eating much grass, but he's trying; dear of him) and is hopefully learning some horse manners! Tom is feeding really quite well at the moment, still on the milk formula and milk pellets with the Probiotic at night. So the last milk feed is at 11.30pm and the first one is between 6 - 6.30am. It will be interesting to see how things go when he has finished the Probiotic. Ben, one of the vets, rang yesterday; a true Aussie! Just for an update; they have been so good. It's cost us, but without them, he wouldn't be here. So thanks guys!

The Worming!

Well, it's worming time again; every 13 weeks to be precise, and everything gets done! Storm, one of our 12 month old Rug rats (Shetland, but she is just losing her winter fur at the moment, and looks a state) will eat anything and is a real juvenile delinquent! So she was fine. Tilly, our other Rug rat, was a nightmare — she is not collar broken, so we couldn't just squirt it in her mouth. So Laura finally, tediously, loaded apples with worming gel. This took forever; too much gel and she wouldn't eat it; still its done now! Duke wouldn't eat it either, so I tried to give it to him on apples — what a performance; he coughed and spluttered and rolled his tongue about — he hated the taste — what a drama queen. Finally he pinched Marble's, so he had 2 lots; oh well. Marble also had to be hand fed apples with gel. What a game that was; it all took a good hour or so! And then there was Tom; his first worming experience! The measures are geared up for 100kg plus, and he is only 10kg or thereabouts! So the smallest bit of gel was administered, and he even gave us a cuddle afterwards; if only they were all like him!

Monday 11 June 2007

Tom needed a bath!

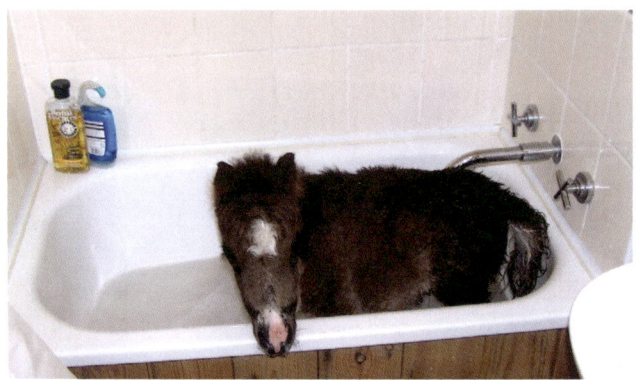

It's a good job the weather has been so good recently. Well, Tom was doing really well; I thought we had cracked it! But Saturday evening the runny botty started again. I really thought we had got through all that; he is still on the Probiotic and same feed routine, but he was so bad yesterday he had to have a bath! He was washed and scrubbed and fluffed up after; I don't think he liked it that much, but looked a lot better for it! I think a phone call to the vet may be needed; let's hope we get through this (another) setback.

Poppies before the pigs!

Well here is the proof that we did in fact have poppies, until Rosie, Daisy and Oscar got out! They ate the pink roses, poppies and all my blue forget-me-nots that I had grown to make a blue carpet of colour. I can't believe those pigs!

Tom meets Lulu, alias Flopsy

Poor rabbit; we are torn between calling her Lulu and Flopsy — she seems to answer to both, so I guess its OK. Well, Tom had his first rabbit kiss; they are quite fond of each other. I may get a little pen and put them both in! I cleaned out the guinea pig and rabbit cage; made an upstairs in it now! Thought I may paint it at some stage; little chimney, letterbox etc — wish I had time!

Tuesday 12 June 2007

Billy meets Mummy Monkey!

One of the young chicks was being picked on by all the others. It was the youngest of the brood, and he/she was getting it in the neck (pardon the pun!). We rescued it and put it in a cat box with straw and a new fake mum (Steven's hairy monkey toy!). I really didn't think it would make it through the night, but I gave him some warm weetabix and put him to bed. In the morning he was still there, cuddled under the monkeys arm! So more weetabix for breakfast and chick crumbs for lunch; I think he is doing quite well. He must be lonely though, but I am afraid to re-introduce him as they may finish him off ...

Wednesday 13 June 2007

Lucky—what a star!

Lucky, our Springer, who is a real pain; cute but a pain, ate all 10 of my new solar powered lanterns. She ripped them out of the ground and crunched the glass, and all that was left was the black cap with the light! I thought: not having this; bought those lights and I am going to use them! So I tied bits of wire to them and hung them around the garden; in the trees, on the arch — wherever it was high enough to not let Lucky finish them off! See: 1-0 to Michelle! Never be beaten!

10 steps forward, 25 steps back

Well Tom has still got a bad tummy. The vet suggested electrolytes, so we are giving him them for the next 24 hours; no milk! Ah poor Tom; he loves his milk. But we have got to try something; I need to bath him again later, to make him more comfortable. He has lost a fair amount of fur on his backside due to being so poorly. We are using cream to help any further damage, but it's not going to get better until his belly is sorted. The weather isn't so good at the moment, but I will clean the shelter later and give him some fresh straw. That might help; who knows?

Walter Bailey came!

Walter Bailey arrived with the hay. He offered to take a look at the pigs for us, and guess what? Good news — Rosie and Daisy are mums to be, and by the looks of things, it's not going to be long! I have no idea of when they last returned, so it could be any day. We have got so much to do — partitions to build, sections to redo, gates to re-hang, bars to be made and installed, pigs to be separated — aaahhhh — more feed needed, more bowls; oh, we have really got to get our skates on and get sorted!

Thursday 14 June 2007

The pigs nearly won!

Well what a day — drove the car into a bollard! Jeep failed MOT big time, then I came home, not a happy bunny. But all was better when I saw Pete; I just couldn't stop laughing. I came in the door and he was stood there as if nothing happened; he was black with mud from top to toe; then the story came out: he was putting in the pig bars

ready for the piglets, but they were heavy, so he opened the gate to get through. The 3 pigs pushed their way out past Pete, knocked him flying. Whilst he was picking himself up, the pigs found the pig nut bin and were all in it; a huge dustbin full of feed — they must have smelt it! In a panic, Pete tried to get them off, but they are hefty pigs and not easy to shift! So he wrestled Oscar the boar to the ground; lucky Oscar didn't kill him! Whilst rolling around on the ground with a boar the other two decided to investigate. Pete seized the moment, jumped up, grabbed the bin and ran. Once the bin was safe, he went back to put all the pigs back in. I wished I had seen it; by the look of Pete it was some fight!

Sunday 17 June 2007

Short back and sides!

Well the farrier came today to pamper Duke! He had his feet trimmed; this occurs every 8 weeks or so. Duke isn't the best at standing still, and he is fairly old now, 20 in fact! So his legs don't bend like they used to! But good result; he felt much better after a quick cut. Storm wasn't so easy, we had to use ropes, collars and a twitch, and she still was a strong little thing; she is only 12 months and I would assume this was her first run in with a farrier! It has been a long while since the farrier perspired like that! I think we will attempt the wilder ones, Tilly and Marble, next week! Give him a rest!

RSPCA fundraising

14/06/2007

Steven had a fundraising thingummybob at school on Friday. They had to dress as something beginning with the letters of the school. And you will never guess what he went as; yep — a cowboy! Fancy that; must run in the family! We really are going to have to get this sorted!

Tom is off the electrolytes

Tom is much better at the moment. I have finished the electrolytes and he is back on the milk, every 3 hours, except at night when the feeds run at 11pm, with Probiotic. Then milk pellets until 7am. This seems to be working well at the moment; no runny botty at the mo! So we have another step forward again!

If pigs could read, we'd all be OK!

In my wisdom, I thought I would buy the pigs a bowl each, as they now have to be separated at night in case one goes to farrow (we don't have any dates so it could happen anytime really). Off to Walter Baileys I went — Bonny and Clyde behind the counter (Adam and David that is!) I found the largest dog's bowl I could find and took it to the counter. They asked: have we got new dogs? I said no! They said what's the bowls for, then? I said the pigs; well they were nearly rolling on the floor laughing. See, the best thing is: I was serious! I make such a fool of myself when I go in, I just haven't got a clue; they must think I come from a different planet! (Actually ...) So they furnished me with these bucket things and said that this would be better! I really don't know where I would be without them! We would be in a right state here. Mind you, if you can't make people laugh, whats the point?

It's Father's day

Pete was in his element today, Fathers Day, and guess what the kids bought him, amongst other things? Yes, you guessed it — a cowboy hat, and a lunge whip! Laura and Steven are just encouraging him really! He's in his element; hoof pick in hand and off he goes! Anything is possible with the hat!

Wednesday 20 June 2007

Today, recycling took its toll!

I thought I had better update the signs for the recycling, as I am not sure if people are used to recycling the way we do it in Cornwall: washing and squashing etc. Typed them up, laminated them, ran out to put them up — a huge gust of wind came and blew them right out of my hand. I tried to save them; I leaped over the wood pile, ended up in it; the pile slipped (and if you know where that wood pile is you will know its a big drop!) I caught only one sign, and then fell, not so elegantly, down to cottage 5. Signs? who needs 'em!

My Oracle! Becs at Walter Bailey!

Well, we are having a right game with these ponies! As I said before, the farrier came and it was a bit of a nightmare. Tilly and Marble, the wild ones, need to be broken so we can tend to their feet; it's for their own good, or we may have to find new homes for them. We have tried long and hard, and so far only managed the head collar, and that wasn't easy and we certainly can't catch them to take it back off; we need help! and quick! Off to see Becs — she knows everything! I tried to extract every little bit of advice from her experience that I could. I will try what she suggested, but not being experienced in ponies, it may not work! She is extremely busy, but may be able to just come over and assess how big a problem we may have, and go from there; talk about learning quick — watch this space!

Oh, and plank comment of the week!

I was explaining my day to Pete, and was talking about someone that used to run a Livery and they may be able to assist in our current problem! And do you know what he said? What a plank! He said they won't be able to help, they only work with books! And he thinks he's funny; we have a serious issue here!

PS: anyone who is experienced in horses and wants to give me some advice? More than welcome!

We have a wood store!

Well the wood store is here, built by Pete's fair hand! But he forgot something, I think: wood. It been standing there a while now for people to use the wood for the fire pit; mmm: wonder when it's arriving!

PS the ground is wonky! Not the wood store, according to Pete! Cowboy? mmm ...

Thursday 21 June 2007

Starting to wean

Well, for all you Tommaso-ettes: Tom is still OK and off the electrolytes; so far so good. Its raining like crazy here. Marble, Tom's mum, is teaching him how to shelter at the moment! I did interfere yesterday and put him in the dry, but he must learn how to survive, so must stop fussing! We are starting to wean; this must be done gradually to make sure his weight does not drop or cause any sort of problem. He is now on 4 hourly feeds of 300ml foal feed at 7,11,3,7 and then Probiotic at 8 and put in for the night with an 11 pm feed with milk pellets 50-100gram to take him through the night. This will continue for approx 2 weeks, assuming we don't encounter more problems, so see how that goes. He will gradually take on more grass and this will eventually replace the milk feed all together.

Sunday 24 June 2007

Mobile Mutt!

Looking at Lucky here, you wouldn't believe she could be an absolute nightmare! I left my mobile on the worktop for a while, went to feed horses but told Lucky she couldn't come, and when I got back she was looking a little off colour — out of service! I saw a shiny piece of what used to be my mobile phone on the floor; she had eaten my phone; all my numbers, that I haven't a copy of anywhere else, were now in her tummy! I just could not believe it. Argh. Poxy dog!

Getting closer!

Well, we are trying here! One extremely small step at a time, but we need to break or tame Tilley and Marble, they are so skittish, and as I told you before, I need to get the farrier to tend to them. So Laura started again with Tilley — back to basics, and got her to eat from her hand, and Tilley finally allowed her to touch the top of her head collar; a very small step but at least it's one in the right direction! It's going to be a long job, and may never happen. We'll see.

The pool arrived

The swimming pool arrived, and Laura, our newly qualified lifeguard, was overseeing the whole installation! We thought we would try out a 12 foot round 4 foot deep pool first, then if we use it a lot, we can think about installing a permanent heated pool! I know, I know — no funds, I hear you say, but there is no reason to not look ahead in a positive way. Come on, positive thinking here!

Pool still not full!

The pool had been filling for about 5 hours now and I think our lifeguard was getting a little bored; the attention span was beginning to dwindle, the excitement was dulled ... we didn't like to tell her it would be at least another 5 hours for it to fill completely! Still, never mind — I am sure it's character building!

Pete eases the boredom!

You can always rely on Pete to break up the monotony! He was caught on camera doing one of his little jigs! I hope he has put the stopper in correctly and fitted the pump the right way round or we are going to have to teach the pigs to swim, down on the bottom paddock!

Chicks and Nettles!

Before we could let the little chicks out, Steven and I thought we had better sort the nettles out again. The other weeds were fine and the poppies add a splash of colour to their homes, but the nettles are too big already to battle with, if we have to rescue a chick, when they go out for the first time. Wheelbarrow after wheelbarrow of nettles to the compost heap — we were getting somewhere. It has only been 8 weeks since we did it last; they grow so quick. We tried to get most of the roots out but it's impossible to get them all out. And boy did it rain today, by the bucket; we were drenched several times actually, all in the name of duty — they better appreciate this!

Chick's first day of freedom

Nettles finally cleared; well kind of — chicks at the ready! They loved it, pecking amongst the plants and poppies. We just have to be careful as they are not 8 weeks old yet and may be spotted by the buzzard and made into lunch! They had a few run-ins with the other chickens; there is a pecking order and apparently it takes 2 or 3 days for everyone to establish who is in front of who. There was an awful lot of commotion when we first released the chicks. They had been in the enclosure for a week or so, but not actually allowed to mix directly with the others. We were advised by the famous book (the only one I have, and if its not in there I haven't a clue what I am going to do!) to introduce chicken and chicks slowly to avoid a fight. Billy was also allowed out for the first time but he's more on his own and comes to me to be put back to bed; he is so cute. I can tell them apart but I don't think anyone else could. They have to be put to bed and safe at night; we check on them every hour if they are out.

Monday 25 June 2007

Cockerel Patrol

Our cockerel thinks he's on a mission. I am sure he used to be a Sergeant Major or something. He parades around and tells every chicken who will be sleeping where and puts them in the correct houses! And if one dares to go to the wrong house they are out on their ear! Once all are in bed he takes a final perimeter walk and then retires for the evening. The only trouble is, if you disturb him on this final walk and he hasn't quite gone to bed, he will start the whole routine again, so you have to come back later to shut them in! I wonder if all cockerels are like this, or is he just a control freak?

Yipee, we have piglets!

We fitted the bars to the pig stys and separated them at night, like David had said. This one night Oscar went in the wrong sty, but it was so cold and miserable we thought ah well, leave him there. Rosie showed no sign of milk coming in or imminent birth, so we thought it wouldn't matter for one night! How wrong were were (again!). I came down to feed everyone in the morning, went to place the feed in the first sty and there before my eyes: 8 little pink piglets. I shouted to Pete to come quick — what should we do? Well, we took the decision to move Rosie to the sty nearest the gate, with bars, and then moved the piglets. We thought we would ring David quick and ask him what to do now! But you remember the phone Lucky ate? Well, that was the only place I had Davids number — we were alone! help! Well, we did what we thought was right and managed for the day; David would have to be contacted tomorrow

Oscar got the hump!

Rosie, who had just been through a rather traumatic time, was given a little more feed. Oscar was disgusted he didn't get any! Took his bucket, threw it in the water and then on his head. He ran around with his bucket and chewed the handle up! Not that he likes his food or anything!

Pete the cowboy turns lumberjack!

We need to clear the top bank, so stared at 8am, in the rain; heavy rain! We took down so much bracken and nettles, then a small tree needed to be felled; Pete turned into a lumberjack. Anyone would think it was a 150ft tree; it was barely bigger than a sapling! Anyway he cut it down and chopped our first logs — 3 to be precise! Finished 9pm, in the rain, heavier than the morning. We were absolutely drenched. There is so much more to do, but it was a good start.

How cute are they?

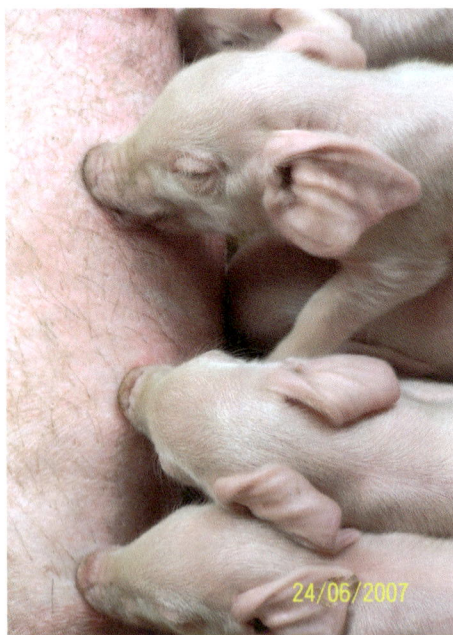

Just couldn't resist this photo — just perfect, 3 little pigs, just nearly one day old!

What a day!

25/06/2007

Monday morning; never a great time in anyone's life! Back to school, back to routines you could do without. Well, I just dropped Steven to school, and as I said before I was going to try to contact David, Bailey that is, to ask about pigs. Well, David must have been reading my mind, he called me first! I popped in to see David and he said we need heat lamps and quick; oooohhhh I hate that "and quick" phrase on the end. So I zoomed to the electrical outlet, got some 2.5 cable to run a line from the summerhouse to the pig sheds, plus plugs and connectors. They didn't give me 2.5 cable did they — oh no, they decided to mess my day right up. They gave me 2.5 connectors and 4 mm cable; mmm nice .... how much of a problem is that? Well when its raining, its a huge problem. I ran the first 50m cable down and tried to connect it up; the rain just emptied, my hands were wet, I was sliding down the slope, the tools were a mess, I was a mess. After several attempts, I lost the little screws. Pete was at a meeting, so I was alone! Off to get a new connector; 2 hours had passed by now! Meanwhile David turns up to cut the piglet's teeth. They are like razors. I tell you, it's a good job he's about; we would be lost without him! Go Dave, go Dave! Well, he told me what to do next: clean pens and remove straw, lay shavings, plug in heat lamp (yeah, like I can do that at the moment!). Well David went, and back to the lamp problem. To cut an increasingly long story short, I finally managed it, hung lamp, laid shavings and Bob's your uncle — job done!

2pm! What a day! Well, half day anyhow!

Tomasso

Tom hasn't really been out in the rain yet. But he certainly made up for it today! I thought he would get cold and bored of the rain; it just emptied all day. Tom was out leaping around in it; he was running here and running there. Seemed to be extremely hungry today too, which is good. I hope there are no repercussions after his wet day ...

Steven puts piglets to bed

All calm now, bedding in, heat lamps still working, and piglets need to be sorted out for bed. I let Rosie have a few minutes outside to stretch her legs. Also needed to put some sanitising spray on one of the piglets that Rosie had stood on really bad. The leg is sliced open, but should heal with some spray, after a few days; if not it's off to the vet! Steven sorted them out and tucked them up for bed. Rosie was back in and fed them their supper …

Tuesday 26 June 2007
Swallows home to roost!

We have been hearing cheeping for a while and wondered where it was coming from. I thought it was in our woods or something, but no, its in our garage. Well, we call it our garage; it's just a huge glorified shed thing, a bit battered, but ours nevertheless! The swallows are nesting in the rafters. We caught this picture today, just as mum was returning to feed the little ones. You can see two here, but I don't know if there are any more. We don't want to get too close, in case mum rejects them. Babies all over the place: chicks, ponies, pigs and now, swallows!

Wednesday 27 June 2007

Chicks—just having a laugh!

Days are always busy here, and I can't tell you everything that goes on, you will think I am really crackers! Whilst I was tending to the piglets last night, Pete was on bed patrol for the chicks! All the big ones were in and ready to be shut in for the night. But (this is allegedly!) all the little ones were running around still. Pete was running around trying to catch them to put them to bed; (Apparently!) he was there ages and they kept playing around and running about. Well he gave up! So when I was sorted we went down to the pen together, prepared for a catching sesh! But they were nowhere to be seen. I opened the lid of the beds and there, looking up at me all innocent, were 6 little chicks. I then looked in Billie's house and there he was, all cuddled up to his monkey!(You would have had to read the story so far as to why he has a monkey!). I think Pete was either going mad or the chicks were just having a laugh!

Adam, our main man!

Adam, our guy that helps us no end (well we pay him, but he's good!) is here today setting out the posts for the front Woodmill Farm gate and the posts that will support a deck around the swimming pool. Weather isn't too bad today, so I think he will work outside all day today and do the inside jobs tomorrow, when the weather's not so good. Adam is the guy that built our field shelter, cupboard and back decked area and he's got a great big list of to-dos for us, poor guy. I had better get on with my drawing work or he won't get paid!

Congratulations again, Peter Hume!

Congratulations are in order for Peter, hubby of mine! And partner in our Purl Design sustainable architecture firm, www.purl-design.com. One of his previous schemes which he designed and saw through to fruition (The Urban Village, St.Austell) has won a National Design Award. Way to Go Pete! Well done, and congratulations.

This adds to the other recent awards, for Pentire crescent, Newquay and Albert Road in Fowey. Well done; lets see what we can do with Purl Design now!

David, pigs and ironing!

See, that title made you read it didn't it? Well, David kindly came tonight and ironed the pigs; no that's not a technical term for something or other. The piglets are now 4 days old and as they are not out on the soil yet, they need an iron injection to help them along. Next time I will have to do it! (yeah right, we'll see!). They squealed a bit and then were marked with a yucky colour green marker to remember who had been done (Got to sort that colour out!). Thanks to David, I didn't have to attempt this first. I guess I will just have to get used to it; David to the rescue yet again! He's going to appear in my book a little more often than he thinks at this rate! (not sure when to write this book; probably the spare hour between 3 and 4 in the morning, but everyone is after me to write it, so I will have to give it some serious thought! God help the proof reader!) Also Rosie, Daisy and Oscar are getting so impatient, I can't even get to the outer gate now before they are jumping over the gates in the sty. Daisy scratched her neck today doing it; the gates are over 3 foot high! Oscar was out too; not sure what to do really. Probably have to rig something up to stop them! Anyone would think they hadn't eaten for a month!

Thursday 28 June 2007

Solar power Steve!

We really need to invest in solar power energy. So off to Bailey's again to talk to Solar Power Steve! He tried to explain the different ways in which we could achieve what we needed; he had a right job on! The power pack with the panels for just the fence is £238, let alone all the solar panels we need to provide power for the heat lamps. We will need a storage battery and all sorts; may have to put that on hold. Why is it so expensive? Perhaps I could invent a cheap option — not sure I want to sit and use pedal power though!

Flying pigs!

What a morning; Pete and I have been down with the pigs all morning, trying to rig something up so they don't jump over the gates. The gates are 1m high; if I hadn't seen it myself, I wouldn't have believed it. They are going to hurt themselves; I don't know what I was thinking of — write a book! I haven't even got time to think, let alone write a book! Still, you got to have goals in life!

Friday 29 June 2007

Becs came!

Last night we had a very welcome visit from Becs, who works at Walter Bailey. She did mention that she would try to pop in sometime to look at how big a job we have on with the ponies! I know she's very busy, so was delighted to see her. What she doesn't know about ponies isn't worth knowing! We went down to the fields to see Marble, Duke, Tilley and Storm (not forgetting little Tom). I think we really have got a huge job on trying to break the wild ponies. I have ordered a gate like Becs suggested, so we can fence off the other field shelter to try and have continuous contact and see how that goes. Pete doesn't know it yet, but he's going to have to hang it later! I'll slip it into conversation!

Pigs still flying!

I can't believe after yesterday that Oscar still managed to jump the fence this morning. We made a visual break so he would think he could not get over. But he just jumped straight through it! When he wants to get out, he will. I think he just wants a cuddle; he's a bit jealous of all the contact we have with the girls really! Well, we are going to try to foil his plan with a bit of 5x1 later!

The Beast of Prideaux Woods!

If you see this beast, do not approach! Mad and dangerous being! Just kidding. Do you remember me telling you about the musicians that came to stay, and Paul promising me a photo of his antics? I couldn't believe it when I saw him. Well, what a week we had with them; I hope they come back — they were great people and we missed them when they went home. It just shows: at 60 fun is on the cards at every opportunity! Paul, if you are reading this (I told you not to use that hairdryer; look at the state of your hair!).

Sunday 1 July 2007

So that's where they have been hiding!

Each evening when we go to put the chicks to bed, they always play us up. They are like naughty little children. Found a hiding place of theirs though, so may have cracked it for tonight!

Piglets first day out

It was the piglets' first real day out today. The inner gate has been left open for them to explore their outer pen. They are soooo cute. David popped down to see if the little piglet's leg was ok. It's a bit swollen, and he sorted him out. Hopefully he should feel better soon. The piglet that is, not David (I hope he's ok too, but you know what I mean!). Let Rosie out to stretch her legs, but all she seems to want to do is get back to her piglets; she's a good mum!

Fooled by a pig!

Well it won't be the first time I've been fooled by a pig! But Daisy took the biscuit. I was waiting any day for her to farrow; everyone thought the same — she had changed shape, put on weight. I was looking after her with kid gloves. And then she dropped the bombshell: she is not in pig, she has just returned! No wonder Oscar has been breaking out of his pen; he is looking for her. Still, we will keep an eye on the dates and go from here; at least I should have a better idea now! I don't believe it!

Monday 2 July 2007

We have baby moorhens

We have had at least one resident Moorhen for a while now, we just thought he had adopted us and was enjoying the duck feed; he was always around at feeding time. Well yesterday, I was feeding the ducks when I saw a tiny black fluffy thing zoom across the water. I kept watching and the mum came out with 4 other babies. I have never seen baby Moorhens before. I hope the rats and buzzards leave them alone; they were all happy just pottering around in the pond. The babies make a right racket! Just hope they are still there ...

Tom's first feeling of rope!

Tom is now 10 weeks old; time flies doesn't it? Although he is not weaned yet, it is important that we start to get him used to a rope around his neck in order that later on we are able to put a head collar on and lead him. We are also doing his feet everyday, he hates it but he will get used to it in time, I hope!

The rope was just placed around his neck; well, you would think we were doing something really horrible to him — what a fuss. Even more reason to keep doing it! He won't be lead on the rope he will only move with my hand behind him gently pushing him. I think he's going to be a right one!

The Probiotics had finished, but the vet has put him on another tub so it should cover him for the next month or so; he's not doing too bad at the moment.

Becs came with backup!

After the initial 'have a look' at Tilley and Storm, Becs returned for some serious business; Dave came along too. After an hour of chasing, they finally got Tilley into the field shelter. I think Storm had eaten a bucket load of nuts! By the time Tilley had got in there ... she is so fast, once in, Becs got in with them and told us what to do now. So off to Baileys to get more electric fencing to create a little paddock to handle them, and we need another power pack, so I have ordered a solar power fencing kit (from solar power Steve!). If it wasn't for Becs, we would be in a right state. At least she will be able to guide us through the next step, and then on from there. The trouble is, when you are unsure of what you are doing (putting it mildly!) it's good to have an expert on hand. I think she should set up her own business doing this sort of thing! Or Internet help line or something! So thanks, Becs and Dave—so far so good!

Trying to get close to Tilley

Shelter secured, so thought we would start the process of breaking them! Laura got in with them and tried for a couple of hours to get them used to being confined with a person. They seemed fairly relaxed, and Storm will help this process, as she is more approachable than Tilley; hopefully Tilley will learn from her. The next step really, I guess, is to get them used to touch and eventually on a rope (that seems far away right now!)

Trying to unravel the fencing wire!

We have had a very busy morning here! Laura and I have been unravelling electric fence tape for what seems an absolute age! I did put it away neatly so this wouldn't happen, but Pete has been in the shed and dumped a load of stuff in there, and now its a right mess! Cheers Pete! As soon as it's unravelled, we can sort the paddock out!

Yippee Doo!

At last, we have an electric fence, all built and sorted out by our own fair hands. Ok, ok, I know its not difficult! But you should have seen the mess of the tape, it took forever. Well let's just hope this small area will be enough to give the ponies enough fresh air but not too much room to bolt. We will start the handling process tomorrow now; just let them get used to the fence for a mo!

Ponies try out the new paddock

Tilley and Storm were let out, and seem to enjoy their new restriction paddock. It wasn't too bad for them, they seem to remain quite calm. I hope we can get them back in tonight though, as I need to charge the electric fence battery; the solar power one won't be here for a week yet! They have water and hay, with a small amount of grass in the paddock which we will keep an eye on, see if they need extra feed; they should be fine though. So far so good!

Tuesday 3 July 2007

Becs on hand to get a lead on Tilley!

Becs arrived today to say hello to Tilley and to see if Tilley had forgiven her for the other night! Storm was fine, Tilley a little nervous, but was ok. Things were going really well, so Becs took the plunge and got hold of Tilley's head collar. After quite a struggle, she managed to hold on; it was like a rodeo. I am glad she is around, I don't know if I could have done that. You need to remain calm! So, after a while just talking to Tilley and calming her back down, we put on a piece of string to help us hold onto her when we try the same tomorrow. And real bonus: Pete and I managed to clean out all 4 of Storms feet, first time. Well impressed! Things are looking up. So that's Storm, Duke and Tom's feet that are being done now. Result!

Making bread!

In my hectic life, I miss the "making buns and bread" thing for the kids, so I thought I would slip in half an hour and do something for them, like they were used to before all this madness happened! I hope one day I will have a little more time, half hour would be fine, just to catch my breath! Well I bought this bread maker; never used one, always wanted one! Easy, they say: just chuck it all in, they say — it does it all for you, they say, and then Bob's your uncle. Yeah, right! I put in the ingredients, closed the lid, went about my work for half an hour and came back to dough factory. The dough was rising out of the lid and down the sides. I peeled the top back and tried to scoop the mixture into a tray to resemble rolls, to save wasting the sticky goo. Then left it to rise; well, it did the same again. I was in a right mess. The thing was going mad; I had it everywhere, and then there was a knock on the door. I tried to act all professional with a hand full of gook behind my back! Mmmm, bread makers. Who needs 'em? Pardon the pun!

Sunday 8 July 2007

Moorhen family day out!

Until now, we haven't really seen mum and dad out together with all the babies; they are a little camera shy. I sat patiently (if you know me, you will know that's very difficult!) waiting for them to come out and managed to get some great photos of them. Their feet are so big compared to their bodies, they almost look like two different birds stuck together, and they run like cartoon things. So cute!

The taming of the Tilley!

Still working on Tilley, I think it will be a very slow process. I wish you could just do a week of work with her and then job done, but no! She's going to take forever to calm! Although Laura did manage to get a kiss out of her! She doesn't seem to get close enough for you to get your weight behind it and grab her collar in the field. It will be worth it in the end!

The new mini-tractor came!

You remember the ride-on lawn mower we bought a few months back? Well, that had to go back! It just wasn't man enough to go up the incline it was bought for, so we upgraded it to this little beauty! It is 21 bhp, so we are hoping this will be enough to go up the hill with a trailer of dung! (ok, ok, too much information there!) or logs or something heavy. It has a trailer, or grass collection facility, and chain harrow attachment etc — hopefully this is the one! No idea how to work it yet!

The sun arrived!

Took a picture of the lovely blue sky! We haven't seen it in a while so, in case it disappeared too quick, I took this as a brief reminder of what it should look like in July! Mind you, we have got away with it lightly really, compared with further up the country; they are flooded!

Pete in a tangle!

We are having the trampoline and pool put on a decked area at the mo, and if you recall my fiasco with the wiring and pigs; well this cable had to be moved, which I knew was going to be a nightmare, as I hadn't laid the cable straight or that well (it was raining!). Thought it may be a Pete job! He was there for hours untangling it all; there is approx 100 meters of cable and a dodgy joint in the middle. As you can imagine, he was none too happy! But he managed. Mr Fix it Pete. It now runs happily under the trampoline!

Solar power Steve came up with the goods!

Our Solar power fencing thingummybob was here, thanks to Steve! Well, once I figured out where south was, and that I didn't have to shine a torch on it all night when the sun had gone in to work it, I was up and running (just in case you are wondering, yes I am joking!). Wired it all up, and at present I am able to get a reading of 3000 through it; not bad eh? It runs the whole lot at the mo, from the pigs to ducks to restriction paddock, back to ducks, over the gate and into Toms field; a fair way, really! I am going to look into other solar power thingies! (very expensive but good in the long run! pardon the pun!)

Oscar loving the sun

The sun came out for just the one day! Oscar loved it; he was able to make use of his mud bath once again. He only got half in this time; its not as much fun without his girls! Don't panic Oscar, they will be allowed out to play soon!

Adam (a game keeper, you know) came to the rescue!

Adam: he's a star — always happy; he's great. Off to Bulgaria on some mission or other, but before he went, he kindly dropped in to sort out a couple of cockerels (which I really appreciated) and relocated them. The chickens are a lot happier now; all is calm in chicken land for a minute. They only have one leader now, and things are a lot happier!

Weather is very changeable at the mo!

08/07/2007

Not sure what to wear; it's sunny one minute, and thunder and lightning the next. Pete thought this photo was highly amusing and I am being pressured into sharing it with you! Sorry! I look like I have been hit by lightning whilst being dragged through a hedge backwards. You never know; might start a new trend! Mmm, think not!

Mrs P hen came to stay

Not sure when or how our new guest arrived, but she was there, in amongst the chickens! She just appeared from nowhere, she hasn't got any luggage, so I guess its just a flying visit (I know, that was poor; just couldn't resist!). I think it's a Peahen, and not a young Peacock? If not, I have given it a complex!

08/07/2007

Lucky has nearly run out of luck!

I have just about had it with Lucky our Springer; today was bad! Not only is she the new Houdini, she has eaten a light, stolen a tasty morsel from one of the cottages on one of her escapades, chased the chickens, and now just eaten another phone. It was on the worktop for a few minutes and she stole it and ate it, then she pinched two tins of beans and ran into the garden and punctured the tins. I can't take any more! She has been walked, and seems to have got worse! I am barricading her in tomorrow; more fences here we come! That will stop some of it!

Monday 9 July 2007

Aahh, that pesky dog!

Thought I would resume normality for a brief moment and bake. I don't do things by halves, so did egg and bacon pie and 9 dozen buns of some description and 2 cottages pies. Went out with Laura to see to the ponies; when I got back there were 2 dozen buns missing — she had eaten the lot, plus wrappers. That's it! This means war. I am rigging up an electric fence in the kitchen, and that should teach her to leave my baking alone! Plus Pete is putting up a fence to keep her in, so the holiday makers are safe with their food too! *Not a happy bunny!*

Yippee, we managed to catch Tilley

Laura and I went to see Tilley today, to see if we could actually catch her without the aid of Becs. We did! We only held her and stroked her for a while, but it's a start. We haven't managed to do this yet, only when Becs was here, so looks as though we are getting somewhere! We will try the brushes and things tomorrow, see how that goes!

Tuesday 10 July 2007

Penelope peahen still here

Well Penelope is getting her feet right under the table here. She's been to dinner with at least two of our guests so far, and has taken tea on the balcony! She knows where her bread is buttered. Let's hope she stays. If she eats much more she will be too heavy to fly!

Becs the guru!

Becs came again today. I'm so glad she is helping us with the ponies (couldn't have done it without her—Go Becs, go Becs!). Well, after my Guru had finished working her magic on Tilley, Laura and I went out tonight and caught Tilley (no not a code for something, it's a pony!), put her on a lead rope and walked her around the field; how cool is that? And it's only been just over a week. See, a plan comes together when you have someone who knows what they are doing! I can design and draw anything you like, but I can't train a horse! But I am learning real fast here and its all coming together. *Ahh, Bisto*

Lucky just doesn't learn!

What is it going to take? Yesterday, I was joking when I said "use an electric fence in the kitchen", but today I am serious; another 6 fairy cakes went for a burton! She's a nightmare. I tell her off, but she's not having any of it; she just runs and hides in Gem's little basket! Mind you, the peahen did put her in her place — too big a bird to handle, that one! Mmm, I am hearing a plan hatching!

Thursday 12 July 2007

Penelope making friends with Sassy!

Sassy just couldn't resist the chance of meeting with such a huge bird! She was there for absolutely ages. Penelope made this weird noise; whether she was trying to speak to Sassy, I don't know, but it looked pretty strange. We tried to entice her into the house, but she preferred the arch in the garden. If Penelope stays, I won't have any flowers or veg left; she is eating them all. Oh, why do we get the nightmare animals? Maybe its Lucky's friend!

Piglets are growing

The 8 piglets are still going strong. They make such a racket when they want feeding. I didn't realise they grow so quick, you can almost see them growing. We have tried and tried to keep Daisy and Oscar in, but they are determined to get out; I am just afraid they are going to hurt themselves when they jump out. I think David sold us Tigger crosses, not pure pig! I have never seen a pig jump that high! Mind you, until we moved here, I had never seen a real pig (of the animal variety), let alone be a pig farmer! (Ok, Ok, I have a long way to go, but I am trying here; bear with me). The piglets were outside yesterday in the little paddock, they were plastered in mud; its been such bad weather that the mud is deep. Probably better to keep them in the pen area; outside, but a little more safe.

Lucky feeling sorry for herself!

Lucky has had a real run of it lately, and was on the floor, looking really sorry for herself; she just needed some TLC. I obliged! I thought maybe she had learned her lesson and turned a corner. I went off to a meeting, and left Pete's mum and brother Martin here alone with the animals for an hour; what a mistake! Peahen was chased by the Lucky; the rabbit was going crazy, the cats were everywhere, and Pete's mum nowhere to be seen! She was up in the summer house, with her head on a footstool and feet on a roll of wire (we are working up there at the mo, having the decking done) asleep! No, this can't be right. I asked what's been going on? She said Lucky was running around like a loony as soon as we left, and she decided to get out the way for some peace and quiet! Is everyone's life this crazy?

Penelope has fallen in love with Lulu!

Now I am not sure if Penelope is a girl, or a young man that hasn't got his long quills yet. He/she was showing off to the rabbit Lulu! She was strutting her stuff up and down for quite some time; I think she gave up when the rabbit was clearly not impressed. I hope she is a girl, as you can't have a boy called Penelope can you?

I have caught her on camera with her tail on the way down, but you can see what she was up to!

Friday 13 July 2007

We are wired up for sound!

After a completely mad day yesterday—have we/haven't we managed to get power to the loft spaces of both buildings? — and pete half knocking me out with a ladder—we finally got everything to work. We are now WIFI ready. This is only possible within the four cottages housed in the Mill—Buttercup Cottage cannot be linked into the broadband without extensive wiring, and my track record proves that this could be difficult!

Becs has got a lot to answer for!

I nipped to Walter Bailey to get peacock food, and came home with a squidgy pig (thanks to Becs!) that makes a snorting sort of noise! Mmm, something wrong there. I frightened Pete. I took it home and cuddled it, and it made a noise. Pete thought I had bought another animal for the ark! It is supposed to be a dog toy! Tried it out with Lucky; she was so scared of it, she slid along the floor and jumped up under my jumper before I could stop her, and wouldn't get out. What a wimp; all the antics she gets up to and she's afraid of a squishy pig!

Monday 16 July 2007

Tilley had the whap!

It must have been the rain or something, but Becs and little Morgan came over this weekend to work on Tilley a little more. Becs thought we would be brave (*argh!*) and take them out of the field on a lead rope. Well, Storm reluctantly got going, but Tilley just wasn't having any of it. It's a good job Becs knows what she is doing. She had to wrap the rope around the gate post to stop Tilley from going completely mad. See, if that was me, it would be me wrapped around the gate post! We finally got her out, stroppy little madam, and she wasn't too bad once we got her out. I think for a moment we will continue to walk her around the field and try to pick her feet up; this out-of-the-field business may be a step too far at present for us learners!

We have gone eco!

We are trying gradually to go completely, well, as far as possible, sustainable. We are recycling, and trying, where possible, to eat our own home grown produce, with no spray or pesticides; just using what nature intended. Frogs for slugs, and lace wings, are the next ones to get hold of. We have solar power fencing, which is a start, and I have just gone over to Ecover, which is a Belgian product not tested on animals, 100% recyclable packaging. Will not harm the water courses, and good for septic tanks, a great environmental product. This product comes from the place where two of our guests live in Belgium. Anthony and Annemarie even kindly brought a bottle of liquid over for me to try; how kind. So we have swapped the toilet cleaner for an Eco version, also the sprays, wash powders and fabric conditioners, so that's all the cleaning products eco friendly. We will work on the next part now. It all takes time, but if everyone does a little, it must help.

Wednesday 18 July 2007

Three inch moth!

Didn't realise how big some moths are. This one is huge: approx 3 inches! Don't know what sort it is though—I haven't found out what that butterfly I photographed was, either. I can't find it in any book, so if anyone knows, drop me a line would you? Thank you kindly! We seem to see a lot of species here that I haven't seen before.

We had some sun!

Summer must be nearly here; we had sun today! Flowers are ready for a little bit of sun; the rain has washed many of the spring and summer flowers out! Never mind, there is always next month! Well, it was great here today, and I am sure things are on the up!

I saved a vole thing!

I know we must have hundreds of these, and rabbits, and mice etc. but I can't help saving them. The cats catch them, so I have to save them and return them to the wild; must be mad! This one was hiding behind one of the boxes in the dinning room with Sassy ready to pounce; she had brought it in to play with. So I wrapped him up and made him better, and now he is happily enjoying life at el Woodmill: deck chair sombrero, little cocktail by the side; oh yes, he is a happy vole!

Penelope came in for breakfast!

Just sitting having breakfast, when there was a tap at the glass. It was Penelope, our adopted Peahen. She is still here, not flown to pastures new, and getting her feet firmly under the table! I invited her into the conservatory—only the polite thing to do!—and she had her Weetabix and Ryvita and thoroughly enjoyed them; not sure what's for lunch, but maybe she will show up again! Mmm, is this normal? I may have lost the plot!

Went to a meeting and came back with runner ducks!

Just a normal kind of day (well, if you can get that here!). Went to do a survey for work. Then I had a text from my brother Tim; he had got a number for runner ducks if I was interested. No hesitation; rang it, went straight from my meeting to get them, came home with 4, at the moment! Might get more! They have a little home now in the pond area, with the other ducks. You need to introduce them slowly, so they have a little house of their own, and a run, so the other ducks can get used to what they look like and sound like without them getting scared. Once all is calm, we will release them to the pond area, and then to the rest of the farm; they can just run around and have fun. Can't wait!

My big man has gone on holiday!

My Main man, Oscar the Boar, has gone on holiday for 3 weeks. He is much needed to see to another lady! He's going to get quite a reputation at this rate! I packed him up with sandwiches for the journey, a little hat, and not forgetting the sun cream and, of course, a suitcase full of essentials! He will probably be very tired when he gets back! We had a bit of trouble loading, running around like looneys, but did it in the end. He didn't want to leave Rosie and Daisy. I may have to visit him to make sure he is Ok; dear of him!

Thursday 19 July 2007
Thanks Emily!

Well, thanks to Emily, who kindly emailed me earlier, I now know what the butterfly and moths are that I posted on our blog. They are both, in fact, moths and the first one is a colourful Scarlet Tiger Moth and the larger 3 inch one is a Privet Hawk Moth. See—ask, and ye shalt knoweth! But only if thou knoweth Emily! I am learning!

Friday 20 July 2007
Runners have settled in nicely!

The four little Runner ducks have settled in really well. We are taking the bigger ducks out for a few days or so at feeding time, just so that the runners can eat in peace as they are still very shy. We felt sorry for them in the run, so released them to the big pond quicker than we were planning, but its a shame to have them restricted. They look so funny when they run. I hope they will become more friendly, like the other ducks. I am sure they will; they are only 8 weeks.

Date

Little fluffy butts!

The bigger ducks eat in the paddock, until all the Runners become more confident. I couldn't resist this photo! I am glad no one captures my butt on camera! Best not come back as a duck eh?

Pete posted through a shoe rack!

Well, when we moved here we had a lot to do, so plans are continually changing as to what we are going to do with the spaces and things here. They tend to evolve as we need the areas. Well, we had a boot room built and still haven't managed to sort the insides; got a few kitchen base units for storage, and a couple of cut-down shelving units for shoes, but no floor or electrics yet; just isn't time. We are not really used to working like this; we tend to blitz it and rebuild, but for time and money on this massive project it's going to take years! Well I will stop babbling now! There was a cupboard originally in the cupboard (a small one) which we half blocked off. I left a few bits in there, didn't need them, no, surely won't need them? Well, last night I needed them! So, lured Pete into the cupboard and pointed to what I needed, and he said "Oh what? You can't be serious—I can't get that" Well "can't" is a naughty word in this house. There is no such word; you just need to find a solution, that's all. So, proceeded to post Pete through the gap in the shoe rack. I nearly died laughing; I got him stuck! Half in and half out; like to have to explain this to the fire brigade! He finally got in, then to get out took forever; eventually, he got out head first and was dangling for a while! So never under estimate what you may need and don't build a cupboard in front of it!

Got the other four runners!

I keep thinking about the Runners I had left behind, and then Pete gave me an in! He said "do you think the rabbit's lonely?" I know, a bit obscure, but I went in search of a female guinea pig; none available for a day or so, so couldn't come back empty handed, now could I? I had been given the go-ahead to get more animals (well kind of), so Laura and I went back out to Tregony and collected the rest of the Runner family. The others were extremely pleased to be reunited. So there you go: another present for Pete—Lucky man!

Bought a chicken house from Bailey's!

Bought a new chicken house for the little chicks that now need a proper home. It is so cute. But when we finally got it to the chicken area, the house wouldn't get through the gate *and it's heavy!* After a long while of trying to get the house over the fence. But I was neither tall enough or strong enough to lift it above my head without laughing! But then brain kicked into gear: its triangular, so if we turned it upside down we wouldn't have to lift it as high. What a plank. Got it in, and put it on four logs to make it better for cleaning, and made log steps to the front … ahhhhh cute!

Tom meets Tilley and Storm

Tom still not as good as he should be on a lead rope! But thought we would take him to Tilley's and Storm's field. He did quite well really; a little shy, but was ok when Pete sat with him. He will have to get used to them at some point, but will have to do this very slowly!

Chicken house in place

Finally got the chicken house in; all sorted—bedding in, ready for the chicks. Spent a fortune on this, and do you know what? Those chickens just piled in the smallest house, all but Henrietta, who was in the other old house! I can't believe it; they must have been like sardines in there. Tonight I will make them use this new home; I mean, it's not like they got to hoover after or anything! It's a home! I must tell you this, its so dippy! There is a block of wood on the top of the house with a ridge in it. There didn't seem any logical reason for this, so I thought aah, there are people like me! I was going to make a sign for the name of the house and put it in this purposed made ridge! Ah, but no: this is the ridge that you put the string in to hold the door up. Mmm, worried?—you should be!

Chainsaw Steve!

Got a great little machine—petrol chainsaw, with a small blade so that I can use it easily. Steve kindly put it together at Walter Baileys, without a hitch. Mmm. I cycled down to there with Gem, our dog, in the back. She goes miles in her little trailer—she looked after the chainsaw until we got home; even got a box of carrots for the ponies in too! Glad David didn't have the 25Kg piglet nuts in; might have had a technical hitch there!

Sunday 22 July 2007

Ours now!

I am trying to make an access from our land to the historic Prideaux Woods. I found a path that I can join on to, but it is completely blocked by overgrown shrubs, brambles etc. That's an understatement! Its real bad! I telephoned the Council, who said they didn't own it, the Wildlife Trust owned it. I phoned the Wildlife Trust and they said Restormel owned it. I rang Restormel, and they said the Council owned it. So, I thought blow this; I will just clear it, and then I own it! So, after an hour of chainsawing the new chainsaw broke! So did it with a hack saw! We are now half way down the path, but it has taken 22 hours so far! I am determined to get to the end; it will be a great place to walk, like a secret entrance to a woodland walk. I need a bridge though, to cross the leat. Have to work on that!

Sorry Steve D-M!

Sorry Steve, just read your reply about the privet hawkmoth; thanks for that, I will check the replies sooner in future! I have just worked out that I can reply to all your comments! So watch out I am here waiting! Here's a picture of a dragon fly that came to see us—any ideas on that one?

Monday 23 July 2007

Who's in Lulu's bed?

Opened Lulu's bed today and found a stranger in the camp! I am not sure whether Lulu lured him in, or whether he hopped in on his own! (sorry!) But he wasn't going to get out; he even posed for a photo; he is a quite a toad, not one to be argued with! I cleaned Lulu out and he settled back in to the comfy warm straw. Don't think he's going anywhere for a while. Talking about strangers in the camp, Penelope has taken up residence with Tom in the field shelter. What a crazy place this is: peahens in with ponies, and toads in with rabbits!

Trixie's first day at Woodmill

Milky, Lulu's friend, passed away a few weeks ago, and since then Lulu has been lonely, so we have been waiting for a female guinea pig to come along, and today was the day. Trixie, an 8 week old guinea pig, met Lulu for the first time; we will just let them get used to one another today and see how things go—hopefully this is the start of a long relationship!

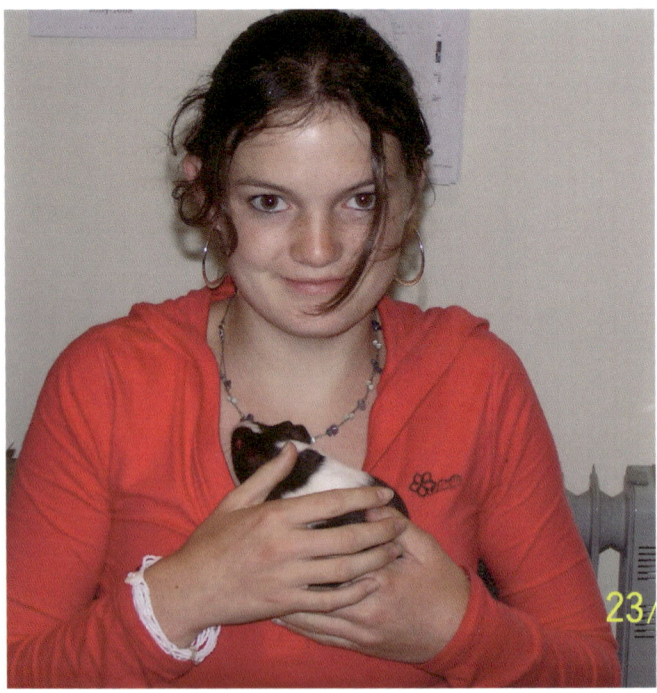

Thursday 26 July 2007

Tom is doing well

Tom, dear of him, is doing really well at the moment. Him and Duke are best of mates! We thought it was about time Tom had a night on the town and stayed out all night! We left his stable door open, so he was free to come and go all evening and bring his friends back. He seemed to like it, but you can't beat a bit of home comforts! He returned to his hay and slept as usual. I think Duke relies on him as much as Tom relies on Duke

Nearly got a pathway!

After days of clearing and chainsawing, we have finally found the path, and where it meets the Prideaux woods. All we have to do now is make a path at the back of the holiday cottages, and a few steps, oh, and a bridge, and a few more steps and, oh yeah, cut a tree down, and Bob's your uncle—job done! Path sorted. See, not much to do now! I did fall out a tree with the saw, doing this, but it narrowly missed me. The tree just fell on me, so I have got a very sore mouth at the mo!

Piglets' first day of freedom

The piglets were itching to get out of the sty, but it has been such bad weather, they would have got lost in the mud! But it was sunny for a mo, so let them out; they were so funny, running and jumping; I wish they stayed like this forever, they are so cute. I just hope they don't escape! I could waste a lot of time down with the pigs!

Piglets' first taste of pig food

The piglets just don't seem to be able to be satisfied with milk alone at the mo so, after talking to our expert, David, we gave them some pig food behind the bars, so Mum wouldn't get it. They looked like they hadn't ever eaten before; they were in it like a shot. The one pictured above had just come out of the bucket. You just want to sit and watch them really; better than TV! (mind you, still haven't watched TV since the 16th Jan!)

Laura in hospital

Bit of a nightmare. Laura, our daughter, is in hospital for a bone operation problem. She had her leg operated on yesterday, but all did not go quite according to plan; she had to stay there last night, and I am on the way back down now. She collapsed twice. I hope she is better today. The docs think she will be out of action for 3 -4 weeks—aahh, I will have to do all the cottages without her; that is a nightmare, as we are quite a formidable team! Never mind; just hope she gets better real soon ...

Sunday 29 July 2007

Mum and Steven to the rescue

Not only have I not got Laura at the moment as she is recovering from a knee operation and needs constant care at the mo, my aunt from Spain has had to cancel her stay in the UK. She was going to be a fill in! (probably that's what put her off! Still, we will get her in November, she won't get away with it!) Luckily for me, mum offered to help clean the cottages as I have not got Laura to help at the mo. Steven even got in on the act and polished all the cottages as we cleaned down through them. So clean team to the rescue—thanks guys!

Saw a hare!

We have got plenty, and I mean plenty, of rabbits here, but never seen a hare. At least, not until yesterday. I didn't realise they were that much bigger than rabbits, and a totally different shape face. There is a wildlife website that you can log your sighting so they can track the hare population; I will have to find it!

Tuesday 31 July 2007

The Farrier came!

Well, the time was here; after an intensive 4 weeks with Becs and us doing the necessary foot picking and catching etc. it was farrier time … dun dun duuuunnn … He rolled up in his red van and strode across the field like a cowboy in his chap-like things, to get to work on those pesky little Shetlands. Thought we would start with Duke, you know, the quietest one, the 20 year old that has had this done probably a hundred times; yep, Duke is the man … well, what a nightmare. He reared and bucked like never before, kicked Becs in the chest and the farrier in the nose, but they held fast and his feet were completed, albeit a real battle. I was worried for a moment that he wouldn't do the others. I had told him that Duke was the best one! Well, nothing could deter Pete (the farrier that is!). He did Marble; a little commotion, but not so bad as Duke, and then onto Tilley and Storm. All 4 completed, and just need to book him for 3 months time now! Hope he will come back! *Big thanks to Becs!*

Storm showing off her new feet!

Always the attention seeker is our Storm. She had her feet and hair done, and it was all out to show the world how good she looked. Rolling on her back with all four hooves in the air! I really need to have a word with that girl!

Next step to our pathway

We have been busy clearing again, and are now ready to build a bridge, then the steps. Probably a few weeks off completion, but it's getting there. Here is a picture of my favourite tree; it reminds me of those trees you would play in as kids, pretending it was a foreign land (not much has changed really has it!)—which I will be able to see with ease after the bridge is formed and installed. Watch this space!

What a lovely day!

About time isn't it? The weather has really been missing these last few weeks, but it's here now, and I hope it's going to stay. The flowers are back out, and there is grass where the mud used to be! Just a perfect kind of day. I took a picture of the tranquil picnic bench; this is where I aim to be sitting at some point this year! Let's hope eh? Just a few minutes would be nice …

Put a stop to Lucky's antics

After a nightmare of a day, I had popped out for a few minutes to get pain killers for Laura (she is out of hospital, by the way, and recovering well; she still will not be able to help me until at least the end of August: nightmare). Well, I was only gone a few minutes and Lucky escaped. She ran into cottage 4 and stole a flip flop, (luckily, they are really nice people!) into Cottage 3 and stole a phone charger, and gave them a gift of a mouse (dead!), and generally caused havoc, then rolled over to be loved! Luckily, all items were returned unhurt, but this had to stop and it had to stop now. So Bailey's here we come; got posts and pig fencing and staples; not to put around lucky (although we felt like it!), but to barricade the bank where she is getting out. She is stopped — well for the time being anyway!

Steven the acrobat!

The sunny weather and golf for 5 days straight must have gone to Steven's head; he was flying around on the trampoline like a mad thing; he had to keep his socks on as after a while it hurts your feet. I didn't get as far as a hand stand, just a few swivel hips and seat drops. The decking is a great addition in the summerhouse area—thanks, Adam!

Tom meets Tilley and Storm for the afternoon

Took Tom to see his big sister Tilley and friend Storm. They had a ball; well, Tilley and Storm did; they were chasing Tom around like crazy, only poor Tom wasn't quite sure whether to play, or to keep running back to me for safety. He was bucking and shaking his head; he got tired fairly quick, but I guess he is only 14 weeks or so. He is back on 4 feeds of 400ml and then at 11pm we shut him in to give him milk pellets; he only was allowed out on the town for a couple of nights, but even in that short a time, he lost some weight, and he needs the weight to grow strong, so we will leave it for a while longer and try again; we need to monitor him closely.

Steven waiting for a dip

31/07/2007

The weather is just perfect for a dip in our pool; now the decking is finished, it's just right to jump in at the end of the day. Steven was waiting patiently; he looked like some kind of cartoon character crossed with the godfather! He won't thank me for this picture when he is older! But I have it and I am going to use it!

Storm leading Tom astray

Storm was leading Tom astray; you can see her whispering in his ear to give Pete a nip! He is trying to block a hole that they escaped out of earlier. I think Storm is going to lead Tom into bad ways! The trouble with Tom at the moment is that he is only tiny and is trying his best to eat grass, but it seems to be that difficult for him that the grass sometimes escapes his mouth in the form of green goo! And thats what he greets you with, all up your legs; Mmm, nice!

It had to be done

Probably left it a bit late in the day to have a swim as the air had turned chilly, but we sold it to Pete and he was up for it. Took the cover off; it's not heated but the sun had warmed it up a little; a little insulation may help, have to work on that theory! Well, the top 2 inches was warm, and we said to Pete aahh, it will be ok once you are in because all that 2 inches on the top will warm the rest of it. Yep, he fell for it hook, line and sinker (sorry!). After posing like the man on the mouse trap game, you know the one; the game that everyone had as a kid, and the ball hit the see saw, and the man jumped in the bucket—see, I knew the memories would come flooding back to you! Well that guy; I am still trying to persuade him to let me put it on the blog; we'll see what we can do! You got to see it! Pete got in; fair play to him really, it was absolutely freezing. We put the water games in and had a game or two; we were just seeing how long he would last. Steven tried and failed to get in, which is unusual for him. Laura is out of it for obvious reasons, and I am just a wimp! But we played with Pete, us on dry land and him freezing his bits off! All in the name of duty!

Wednesday 1 August 2007

Beware all of you who use Internet Banking

Well I really have had it! I always trust everybody and have always done so. I never believe that people could be devious and thieves. But I was woken up and had a sharp burst of "smell the coffee" today, when I checked my bank details on line to transfer money to pay bills, when I noticed the account was bare! Some thieving little toerag has pinched *all* my money. I have now reported it to the police and Internet fraud. I hope that I get it back; no tea for us tonight! I am having to waste the next week or so cancelling credit cards, accounts, business accounts etc. and re open new. I will never ever use Internet banking again. Beware you good people: do not use Internet banking!

Friday 3 August 2007

New fencing

The ponies seemed to want to escape today, constantly! So maybe they are just getting bored of the same grass area; after all, they have been there for five days now! So I thought I would move the fence and re-do the electric area. Sky, our cat, decided to help. The more I pulled the tape, the more in a tangle she got; she was having a lovely time, but what should have taken me half an hour took one and a half hours of de-tangling! Thanks Sky! All is well now the ponies are on fresh grass.

Chicks on holiday ...

I guess the little chicks are growing up now; about 10 weeks old now (ish). Well, Oscar has gone on his hols, so the chicks thought "why not?". Here they are in the field shelter. Tilley and Storm have been relegated to the outdoors! The chicks were in there nearly all day, just chilling! This place is mad; the animals that is—no sooner have we provided them with nice new homes, they want to try someone else's pad!

Well and truly in the cart!

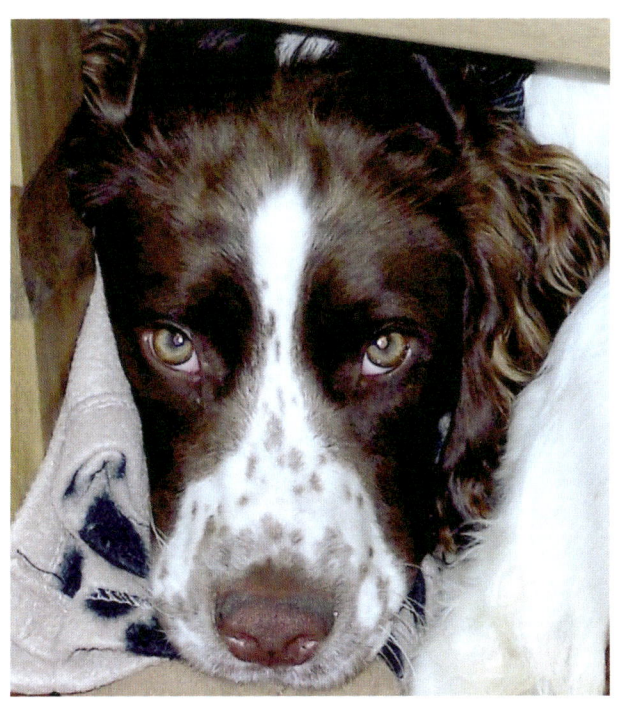

Lucky, Lucky, Lucky; what am I going to do with you? What an absolute nightmare of a Lucky day! We started at 6.30am, when she wanted to go and do all the feeds with us. Thought: no problem, save walking her! No no no, not Lucky; she escaped, and ran toward the chickens. Got the biggest chicken, and secured it in her mouth like a prize possession! With a loud scream, she dropped it, luckily unharmed. She looks at you after, as if to say: "I really just can't help myself—I opened my mouth and it kind of fell in"! Then 8am came. Jeff arrived to help us with some removal of trees. Well, she flooded the floor with leaky Lucky syndrome and proceeded to pinch all Jeff's tools. Thought it was all over by 1pm; we had a client coming to the house, so tried to regain some sort of normality. Prior to him coming, the ponies had escaped once again; he arrived and I was there in my shorts and wellies, looking worse than ever; Pete was sorting the pigs out. Lucky greeted our guests, albeit for a short moment, before being reprimanded and put back the right side of the gate, and yippee do: welcome to Woodmill! Finished ponies and pigs, Pete took control of the meeting, and all was back on course, so we thought! But where was Lucky? I was about to find out when I offered them a cup of tea. Out in the kitchen, where all the fresh eggs for the cottages were (I try to leave some for our guests on a Saturday) was Lucky, looking extremely sheepish. I turned the corner, and there before me was a sea of yellow and egg shells. 20 eggs all over the floor, and none left for tomorrow! I couldn't believe my eyes. Dog, eggs, dog, eggs, client in lounge ahhhh, oh my; what was I going to do? Tried to mop up and appear with tea, as if nothing had happened! My feet were sticky with egg, but at least I had a smile on my face, and resumed the meeting. If only they knew. The day couldn't get much better!

Monday 6 August 2007

It's been quite a weekend!

What a day. We thought we had it sussed on Saturday evening ... how wrong could we be? Finally sat down for a change about 10.30pm; thought we could maybe have a glass of wine or two ... then there was a knock at the door; two 15 year old boys with a couple of dogs that were lost. They said that these dogs had followed them for miles and they didn't know what to do with them. I looked down, and there before me were the two most gorgeous dogs with big brown eyes! They just sat and looked, as if to say: "sort us out please!". I said to the boys that I would deal with them, as it was late and the dogs were black and I wasn't sure what the boys would do with them; they couldn't take them home, and I couldn't have it on my conscience if they were run over. We thought, as we didn't know them, we would put them in the stable overnight with food, water and blankets. No sooner had we got back to the house, they had hurdled the 5 foot stable door and were looking at us through the window! So they had to come in, and we settled them down inside for the night!

Dogs in for the night

Well these two dogs certainly made themselves at home; they found a quiet place to settle in the conservatory and funnily enough, Lucky and Gem, our dogs, were perfectly fine with them; friendly little things!

Penelope the Peahen

We thought Penelope was gone, found pastures new, but no; nothing must be better than the food at Woodmill. She feeds for breakfast with the ducks, and then again for tea with the chickens, and makes an almighty racket first thing in the morning just to let you know that she is here! I think she likes it here. She has taken up perching on top of the greenhouse, and spies on our tomatoes!

Breakfast with Sampson

The morning after the night before! The new visitors (dogs) woke up; they are so friendly, someone must be missing them somewhere! Rang the police, but no luck; rang RSPCA but they were closed, and the dog warden doesn't work weekends. But we were getting quite attached to them by now and thought instead of saying: "you, come here!", we gave them temporary names. The Lab was Sampson, and the springer, Sasha. Sampson wouldn't leave Steven's side, and sat and had breakfast with him! We even contemplated keeping them, if we couldn't find their owners!

Lulu's first taste of freedom!

Lulu is getting bigger now, and asks to come out occasionally. She has her own run with Trixie, but she does like to run around without any barriers on the lawn. We do have to watch carefully, as Lucky could think she is the next meal, as would the cats! But she had a lovely time jumping and springing around the garden; she never strayed far from the safety of her home, but at least she enjoyed it. Trixie was less than happy to join her, so left her in her run ...

Happy as a pig in mud!

Daisy was having a ball in the mud bath. She was a very happy pig; for ages she just wallowed in the mud, rolling and shaking, having a really lovely half hour or so; she sat like this for a while, as if to really savour the moment! Pigs are so indulgent! I tried to move closer to take the photo, and she shook like never before. Have you ever seen the film Beethoven, and the slobber as he shook? Well Daisy did this, but instead of flying slobber, it was flying mud and muck; I was absolutely plastered. I hope no-one was watching; it was worth £250 from "Beadle's About"!

New found friends ...

I think Lucky looks up to Sasha. She's a springer cross, but Lucky follows her everywhere; they want to play constantly, which makes me think they are probably working dogs. They will fetch and carry tennis balls for hours. We did notice Sasha is limping a little this morning and it could be that they have walked a long way and are not from this immediate area. I had another attempt today in finding the owners, but after knocking on what seemed like hundreds of doors, and meeting some very nice and some very odd people, still couldn't find their owners. It's a shame; I can't believe they have been dumped, they are too well looked after really. I will wait until tomorrow and try the vets etc.

Lucky!

I just couldn't resist this photo; she has been fired up all day, running for hours; she's really hyper now! We will miss the other dogs when they are gone—our dogs have really made friends with them.

Learn with Daisy!

The piglets have been out with Auntie Daisy today! Learning how to mud bathe! They sat patiently around the pit and listened intensely! A few of them tried the mud thing, but only managed a snout and the front feet! I am not sure what they thought of it really; they were mesmerised. Days out with Aunts; fun times eh?

The day has come ...

Well, I wasn't happy to hand over the dogs to the dog warden and for them to be kept in a little pen. I tried Radio Cornwall once more, and Pirate, and then rang our vets to check. There were no dogs missing. Then the vet looked back over the last month, and found a chap who had reported two dogs missing that looked like ours, a month ago. We managed to get in contact with him, and our Sampson and Sasha were in fact his Merlin and Bracken hunting dogs. It was such a relief to get them reunited with their owners, so a happy ending for those dogs! Cute though; would have kept them if we couldn't find the owners! Mind you, that would have been a nightmare with 4 dogs!

The bridge is nearing completion

You remember the woods we have cleared, to make a pathway up to the historic Prideaux Woods? Well this is the start of the bridge that will span the leat to enable you to walk easily to the pathway; we only need a few steps, a hand rail or two, and that part will be completed; we then need a pathway from the cottages to the bridge, a few more steps, and a hard standing at the rear of the cottages ... getting there though! Just a few cut fingers, squashed hands and a nifty little fall, but we are nearly there!

Gem on Par beach

Gem is often talked about, but because she is so good, and doesn't really think she is a dog, I don't have many really nightmares to tell you about her. She thinks she is human, and looks a cross between a monkey and a badger really. She is a real star. When we go cycling, she travels in a kind of child trailer that is used to carry luggage; she has a seat belt and cushion, so is very comfortable and really enjoys it. We originally got Gem from a rescue home; she was a puppy, and they told us that she would grow about Lurcher size; how wrong were they? She is a real hair ball no bigger than a Westy. So, instead of running with us, she has to be cycled around! All good fun though, and she's great. I just hope Lucky learns some good ways from her! Please!

Thursday 9 August 2007

Darling buds of May!

Yesterday was a glorious day. Steven had a rare day off in his summer hols; between competition golf and cricket matches, he's a busy person! We thought we would de-nettle the chicken area once again, so gloves on, and wheelbarrow to the ready. It took us 3 hours to sort out; what a nightmare. Then we thought we needed to pick all the apples for apple pie for tea. it reminded me of the programme "Darling buds of May"; I was catching the apples as fast as Steven could pick them; they are really nice; little red eating apples on the big tree. We don't have any cooking apples yet, but have various kinds of eating apples; they will be fine in a pie! We finished up with a drink on a blanket and a game or two; days off are hard to come by. I guess most people wouldn't say this was a day off, but to us, it was; back to work now—ponies, pigs, ducks, hens, dogs, cats, rabbit, guinea pig—all need feeding!

Laura is on her feet!

After hospital, and then being at home for two weeks not being able to do hardly anything and feeling pretty grim, Laura is up on her feet. Still not functioning properly! But at least she can have a short wander around now. Laura is usually so active, this is a nightmare for her really to be confined; never mind, let's hope she continues to recover; I need her back to work with me!

Monday 13 August 2007
Any ideas?

I wish I could photograph everything I see here; it's like a different world, the amount of different beetles and insects, things I have never seen before; quite interesting! Well guys, what's this one then? moth or butterfly? Do you know how mad this place is? We had a client (yes another one! always happens when we have a meeting!) and I heard a shout from the kitchen; all I could think of is the last time, when Lucky had all the eggs. This time it was Steven shouting to me; we had a baby slow worm in the kitchen! Perhaps he just wormed his way past Lucky (ok that was real poor! Sorry!). Quite a cute thing; I have never seen a baby slow worm; they are either really tiny here, or monster ones!

Pete's been busy!

You remember me telling you about our wood store, and the photo of it, lopsided and all that? Well, Pete has struck again. We haven't been able to dry clothes, and have been using the dryer; not very eco friendly eh? So finally got a clothes line. Pete got straight out to do it, all was looking good, until I put the clothes pegs on it ...

Thursday 16 August 2007

It's been a bit of a day really!

Well, started with good intentions of clearing so much of my Purl Design work, it's untrue. I was going to get back on track today! But Lucky and Co had other ideas. Mmm, started at 6.30; went to feed Tom, and Pete went to feed chickens etc. Well, Gem followed Pete as usual. It rained early this morning, so not a nice one! Got back from the ducks and pigs etc, sat to have breakfast. No Lucky. Ahh, here we go again. That's a song isn't it? Anyway, she had got out and gone on a bit of an adventure; greeted a couple of guests in a Lucky fashion, ie they got mucky and Lucky just rolled over as if to say: "I'm lovely!". Put her back indoors, grovelled to guests (they are lovely, and it wasn't a problem luckily!). Gem was missing; found her several hours later, locked in with the chickens; she must have given Pete the slip this morning. It rained in the night, and you know the washing line that I put a peg on and it went wonky? Well now, the peg bucket had filled with water and the line is now on the floor. Still not started work. Pete ran down to put Tom in out the rain and, only Pete could do this: he hurdled the electric fence and got a pole stuck up his shorts! They are about 3 meters apart, but he did it. Yep, that's our Pete. Took a pick axe to chop some bits away before work and his T shirt came off his shoulder and the pick axe went through it. I tell you, Mr Bean has got nothing on him! Finally started work; and then there was the pigs!

Aaah, the pigs ...

Well, still going; we are weaning the piglets at the moment, so they are in a pen all of their own, but it needed cleaning out; tried to do it whilst they were in there, but it just wasn't going to work. I let them out. They are little monsters now;funny, but monsters. Rosie and Auntie Daisy were in the big paddock as she stills wants to feed them really. Washed everything down, it was a real mess, then thought job done; just pop them back in, tuck them up in a nice warm clean comfy bed — *not a chance* — they were not going back in — *not a hope*. I was chasing them around like some sort of loony. Rosie, by this time, was going spare. I just had to call for reinforcements. Pete and his wellies were on hand! Well we were nearly wetting ourselves, trying to get these piglets in; I hope no-one was watching! Then we gave up, and do you know what? The little so and so's just trotted in like nothing had happened! ahhh, I can't even move them because of the Foot and Mouth scare; we are stuck, until they lift the ban!

Tom Tom Tom ...

Tom is doing just fine at the moment; he is on 3 milk feeds now, and milk pellets, and of course, grass. He's getting quite confident. I have spoken to Grandad Duke and asked him to teach him his manners. I think its going kind of ok. Well Tom, our guest Tom, that is, went to see Tommaso. He turned his back on him and Tom bumped him up the backside and nipped his leg. He thought Tom had gone down to feed him. I think it gave our guest Tom a bit of a surprise to say the least ...

Saturday, 18 August 2007

Mmm, nearly a disaster

Well, I was just doing a little burning when the fire whooshed up; I fell back, entangled in a log, and there I lay for about 20mins. until Lucky woke me, licking my face! What a nightmare; I knew, or thought, I had really hurt myself; I couldn't feel my legs at this point, and I obviously passed out somehow. After a while, I managed to crawl to the phone and was, to cut a long story short, taken to Treliske hospital in an ambulance. They thought I was heading for a few months of traction; all I could think about was "have I sorted the children, where were they, did mum know where to pick them all up from?". Pete was at meetings all day so I couldn't get hold of him, and where would the dogs be now? I don't think I had shut the gate. I would have to tell Laura to prepare the bed packs, fudge and cream etc. and feed all the animals. Oh, and the other thought was ooohhh no, the doctor had to take my boots off, and I had been working in them all day and I had odd socks on! But after 6 or so hours, I was finally released, having luckily not broken a bone, just severely bruised the base of my back. I could hardly walk, and had 5 changeovers this morning. Lucky for me, Laura, Hayley and Mum set about the cleaning and preparation; that was such a close shave; imagine if I was out of it for a few months. I can't even go there ... *thanks, clean team* XX

Sunday, 19 august 2007
Lucky strikes again!

It was a bit of a day yesterday! The dogs were ignored for a few hours while we prepared and cleaned the cottages. I am not sure Lucky liked this very much. We returned to the kitchen, only to find the chainsaw hat and guard (ear defenders and hat) in pieces. Pete went absolutely berserk: *"I can't believe that dog; as fast as we can earn the money, the damn* [word altered] *dog is costing us twice as much in repairs!"* Time to keep very quiet when Pete loses it. He doesn't lose it often, but boy when he does, he means business, and Lucky sensed this; she ran away and hid under the chair. By the time he had finished, we all needed those ear defenders! Things gradually eased, and we all sensed that a cup of tea might help! Lucky came ou, in disguise, with that pitiful sorry eye syndrome and a bowl, as if that could make it better! What am I going to do with her? You just can't help but love her, but she's a nightmare!

Thursday, 23 august 2007
Tom and Tom

You remember me telling you about Tom getting a little shock from our pony Tom. Well here is a picture of them both, so you can picture it better. I think Tom has got Tom under control here! Thanks to Nichola, Tom's (human!) mum, we have a picture of them both. Results today, Tom (not that you need reminding of course) so Good Luck; I hope they are are what you need, or better, to continue your aspirations and goals!

Monday 27 august 2007

Steven in disguise

If Lucky can do it, so can Steven, according to Steven. He thought I wouldn't notice if he and Lucky played with the toilet roll, and he blamed Lucky for his fetching look. I think it's getting worse; Steven is supposed to be training Lucky, not the other way around.

Ponies out together

We thought, as we were getting somewhere with the training etc—how would the ponies like being in together for a change? Well, they loved it; they ran and jumped and got really excited, but then the trouble started just like before. Duke is quite protective over his little family, and gives Storm a hard time. Her and Tilley managed to escape and were nearly on the road. Luckily, some of our guests were on hand to alert us, and they were safely returned to the paddock. Someone had obviously left the gate not quite closed properly. That's the trouble when you allow people to go into the field. I may have to rethink that; you tend to assume that people are responsible, but that is not always the case. But at least they are home safe and sound.

Pig herder Pete!

Pete's got in the swing of it all now! We let the piglets out, and Pete thought he would practice his herding techniques so that when we need to move the big pigs, it will be a piece of cake. Well, they ran rings around him. I think they were playing with him really! They are so cute, and they know it. Always up to no good. This morning was funny; went down to feed them, and all but one, who had wedged himself in the pig trough with the food; he wasn't going to move from there! He looked so funny, just a big butt sat quite happy where he loved it most; the others ran out, but not him, he was there for the day!

Auntie Louise is back!

Well, we knew it wouldn't take long before she wouldn't be able to stop herself from coming home for a bit of hard work! It is supposed to be a holiday, but I guess when you live in Spain, hard work is something different. So didn't want to disappoint her; I had a whole lot of work for her to be getting on with—cottage cleaning, de-nettling, clearing; you name it, we had it. But to break her in gently, so she wouldn't scarper to quickly, we cleaned the cottages and then gave her a little treat, in the pool; she taught the kids how to make a whirl pool and other things! See, that's what aunts are for!

Marble and Tilley

Marble is the mum of Tilley, but they have been separated for 4 months now. But as soon as they got back in a field together, they bonded instantly; it's strange how they never lose that. They had a kiss and cuddle and went off together. Tilley just slotted straight back into the mother-daughter thing; odd, but lovely to watch

Steve and Tom

Tom is the equivalent of an 11 year old I guess now! Steven thought he would share a few tricks of the trade with him, and let him in on the whole 11 year old thing. Well, Tom was quite receptive; he followed Steven around like he was joined at the hip! I am slightly worried that Tom may know tooo much ...

Laura has got it sussed!

After so much training, it was great to see that Laura has finally got it sussed with Tilley and Storm. She can catch them in the field, and even hold them both at once. A few months ago, this was an impossible dream, but I think we definitely have got somewhere with these two; just Marble to go, and then a head collar on Tom!

Weedless!

The pond was a real nightmare; full of stinging nettles and docks: nightmare, but we had all sorts of things nesting in the pond, so were unable to tidy it up until now. So, we seized the opportunity and slotted in a clean up, much to Auntie Lou's delight! We were there for days, but after it was done, it looked great, and the ducks are very happy ducks now. I took this photo from the bottom of the pond area; Steven is fishing out all the bits we dropped in. Looks

idyllic, doesn't it? Can't believe we live here! Thanks Auntie Louise; more jobs to come (I hope we don't kill her off with all this hard work!).

What great weather

The weather couldn't have been better these last few days. We have been in the pool everyday lately, at some point. Our Lifeguard, Laura, doesn't seem to have the right idea; she's in it more than out of it! It's amazing how much fun you can have in 4 1/2 foot of water; a rubber ring, a body board and a couple of crazy people! Steven has now mastered the art of surfing on a body board to the other side of the pool. Laura is the rubber ring champion, and Pete, well he's in the middle of it all! Auntie Louise is keeping well back against the side!

Just the weather for a cocktail or two!

Sunrise specials; the kids have got it sussed; cocktails on the terrace! Can't be bad can it? At least he did make us all one, but I have a sneaky suspicion that this is not his first or last one in that comfy sun chair!

Monday 3 September 2007

Pete's having a crisis—the big 50!

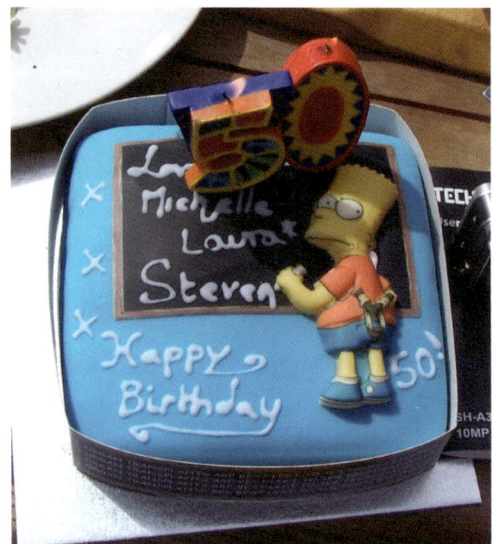

It's here, it's big, it's the big 50! Happy Birthday Pete, you made it! Half a century! I told you I wouldn't let the cat out the bag; just putting it on the blog thats all! Well, we had a pool party, just us 4 and Louise and Doug; bit of a swim, bit of a BBQ, then off to the woods to make an earth shelter; well, the start of it anyway! Dragging logs and chopping stuff; we have made a good start on it; not many people get treats like that on their birthday! Only in this house!

She got out!

Auntie Louise has been working her fingers to the bone here! We have been making paths, clearing fields, pulling weeds, humping stones, chopping logs, digging allotments, poop and scooping—you name it, we have done it this week, making the most of the weather; but this picture is just proof that she did get some well deserved free time in Portloe, pretty little village down Veryan way!

Doug's up for it too!

Not only Auntie Louise that's been working hard here. Uncle Doug has been the grass cutting king! He topped 3 fields and did our lawn; much appreciated, thanks—you can come again!

Rescued another rabbit!

This baby rabbit nearly met with the jaws of doom, but I saved him just in time; how cute is he? I released him back to his friends by the pigs; we must have thousands of them here; I just don't like nature taking its course and the food cycle thing. I try to save what ever I can; sad, I know, but true!

Four piglets get a new home

Well, the pig movement ban has finally been eased, and our 2 families waiting for their piglets were at last able to collect them on Saturday. Alan and Co had 2 boys, and what a game that was to catch them and carry them to the car park area; it seemed like half a mile with a 30kg struggling pig! But they got home safely, and are now re-homed in Cardinham, enjoying the finer things in life! The other 2 girls went just up the road; this was a little easier. Derek parked outside the gate and we loaded quite easily after we caught them; they escaped from the pen! They do make quite a noise when they are picked up and, if you haven't heard it before, can make you quite worried. But they are not hurting or anything; just making a racket. They are also re-homed and happy little pigs. 4 more to go! Want one?

Cool down!

Well, all work and no play makes life not a happy place to be; you got to have a bit of fun in life, and we have to give Louise some happy times, so she will be fooled into coming back! It's been fantastic weather, and the pool has been well used after a busy day; a brief interlude before the evening work commences!

Well done Laura!

Well done Laura, your GCSE results were great. You worked hard and got what you deserved; and on to your place at college for 4 x A levels: Music, Musical Theatre, Music Technology and Maths. 2 years and you will hopefully be where you want to be at Uni, doing a BA(hons) in Music. Well done. XXXX

Monday 10 September 2007

Aaahhh, she has escaped!

Well, two weeks went really quick. Auntie Louise and Doug went back to sunny Spain. They tackled some jobs and we were really grateful. I have a list of 92 and we are on 89 now! Well, that's on the first list anyway! I bet they are laid by the pool, taking it easy; perhaps they might want to live here; they wont be bored then! We are always grateful for any help we can get! Thanks for all the help XX

Sky has been taking lessons from Lucky!

We were late feeding the animals one night; we were just so busy, and they had to wait for half an hour or so. So Sky thought she would amuse herself! Although this photo shows some of the mess, the whole porch was covered in ripped up toilet roll. She was looking extremely happy with herself! Animals eh?

Hens under instruction!

The hens were so funny; they were lined up behind the cockerel, and he was kind of giving them singing lessons; well that what it looked like. I wonder what goes on in their little hen world? The chicks are blending in nicely now, and can hold their own. We are getting about 7 eggs a day at the moment from 13 laying chickens; the other chicks are too young to lay yet.

Sunday 16 September 2007

All change at Woodmill

It's hard getting used to the new times and things at Woodmill. Laura has now started Truro College, and leaves home at 7.30am, so doing the horses beforehand has really gone out the window. She has a lot on her plate, with a heavy Music A-level schedule and Maths; revision and composing takes up a lot of her time, and me being a taxi service takes up a lot of my time! Steven has also had a big change; he started big school (Secondary) this September, and seems to be settling in nicely. He has now committed to golf full time, and is going for county selection. He has had to give up football, cricket and tennis to do this, but its what he wants, so we are completely behind him. He seems to live on a golf course at the mo, and we seem to live in the car parks!

Monday 17 September 2007

Grapes!

We have grapes. We were not sure what to do with the vines, and by the time we realised what we should do, it was too late, so the vines have gone mad this year and only produced small grapes, which is a surprise as we were not expecting them to produce at all. They are really sweet. I picked 3 lb yesterday and am aiming to make grape jelly! Not sure if it exists, or how to do it, but am going to give it a go today! After the wet spell we have had this year, many crops are suffering. There are not as many blackberries around this year, but we did manage to find enough to do a couple pound of jam, and it is lovely!

Bridge opened!

After long hard work, the bridge and access to the woods is finally open! We could do with putting chicken wire on the decking so it is not slippery, and putting in a few more steps to hold the ground firm, but really, it's up and running. The access from the back of the cottages works very well, and really, if you haven't come prepared for walking, you probably wont want to explore up there. You need boots really, and not flip flops, as I found out! But for those who want and like the woods, its a great walk. I think it has added a lot to Woodmill; it's nice to have a secret walk before breakfast, gather your thoughts and gather energy from the trees; aahh, perfect!

Laura and Gem

I think that Gem thought we wouldn't notice her sneak in bed with Laura. Laura is having to sleep in the dining room at the moment due to our German guest. We thought Reka, our guest, should have the nice en-suite room, and Laura the floor in the dining room! Gem found her and snuggled in; good job Lucky didn't find her!

Bounty of produce!

Although it has been a strange year for many crops, we have still managed to produce black currants, red currants, gooseberries, raspberrys, grapes, apples, plums, 1 pear, lettuce, tomatoes, cucumber, beetroot, potatoes, onions, corn, parsnips, extremely small carrots!, green peppers, eggs!, courgets (hundreds!) I think our not so good crops this year; the rhubarb, cabbage, corn; some of the berries are not so good. We have got elderberries and mushrooms, sloes, hazelnuts, rose hips; it's just figuring out how to store everything. At the moment we eat everything that comes in, or freeze it; we haven't really had enough potatoes to clamp, so I have packed them in straw in boxes and use them as we want; seems to be working fine at the moment. I guess we will get in the swing of it. Not a bad start, tho; Dad's been busy!

Wood—you can't do without it!

Well, as my family know, I have a passion for wood; anything wood will do! If I find it I always want to keep it, to make something out of. I never have enough time, so I just end up with hundreds of bits of interesting wood, until we are short, and then it gets burned! This year we must have enough wood for all winter; I spent all day moving it; we need it get it under cover to dry out before the rain comes. I have moved it closer to the wood shed, and separated the small and large; just waiting for Pete to sort the spider infested wood shed so I can get in there! Well, I went to Bailey's and saw the most perfect piece of wood. I talked them into letting me have it! It's huge; I thought it would make a great totem pole. So if I don't get time to carve it, perhaps anyone who is visiting could have a go, and it will somehow evolve; just give me a shout, and I will let you borrow my sculpting tools (so long as you are careful!).

Funny moments ...

We were just here reminiscing over things and, in Petes words: "What a nightmare I am sometimes!". He didn't say "sometimes", but I am sure he meant to! We were renovating a house, and our bedroom was nearly there. I have always wanted a futon, but money was not available, so I set about cutting the legs off our bed! I managed to cut them all off and showed Pete; he was horrified! So I put an extra mattress on it, to bring it up to the right level. That night it was sleeping on a marshmallow bed; we just kept rolling off it. So, still not speaking much, Pete got the tools and bits of legs and screwed all the legs back on, using some kind of double end screw! Poor guy; I think it was around the time I decided to convert our loft and made a hole in the ceiling with a sledge hammer to access the loft. This was no little hole; I never do things by halves! So the loft was about to be converted, plans were drawn up that night, and materials ordered. But whilst it was being ordered, the house was freezing; it was early March, and the snow had just finished! The plastic sheet didn't keep much heat in, and actually flew off whilst mum and dad were looking after the house! Well, I have always believed to seize the moment and go for it in life. You never get anything done by just talking about it!

Thursday 20 September 2007

Found mushrooms!

Well, you never know what you are going to get when you are out looking for a fun guy! Sorry bad joke: fungi! We found this mushroom and the only one I can find in my book (yes, you know the one; the only book I have about this lifestyle, and if it's not in it, we don't know what to do!) anyway, the only one that it resembles is a deadly angel or something like that, extremely poisonous, but can be mistaken for an edible type; any ideas you guys?

The big day has come—Tom is off the bottle!

Poor Tom. I am not sure if we are weening him or us off the bottle; it's been a long hard slog with Tom, but he is worth every bit. It's been so full on, but today he is finally off the bottle. He now eats a mixture of milk pellets and mini pony nut things; we have wedged the gate half open to only allow Tom in, so that Duke won't gobble them all up! Sorry, I have been doing Steven's homework with him, and that bit just snuck in there! Seriously though, Tom's doing really well; 5 months old today—happy birthday Tom!

Grape Jelly

You remember me telling you about the grapes we picked? Well I did make the grape jelly I was on about, and it's really, really nice, so if you are thinking about doing it, it works and it's great. I will try to get my act together next year and make wine! Mind you, I have done that before with rice, plum, parsnip, carrot; well you name it, I have tried to make it! But it was strong enough to knock the vicar's head off, and if you know the vicar, you will understand how strong it was!

Missing his baby!

After feeding Tom for so long, Pete was missing his baby! So we made him one out of a log and coconut (don't ask!) I said I wouldn't put this picture on the blog, but after speaking to one of our guests, they inform me there has not been a Pete picture for a while! So here it is!

Lucky Ahhh ...

I think Lucky knows when to really make my day difficult; what a nightmare. The day I really need my phone, as I am here, there and everywhere, Lucky hunts down my phone, as if to say: "There, you didn't walk me today, you were too busy this morning—now I am going to mess your day up!". She ate her fourth mobile phone. I just can't take it any more! That dog has got to stop! Penelope came in to give her a good dressing down and, as you can see by the picture, she seems to be cowering; maybe it's hit home: *no more mobiles, Lucky!*

Strange animal

Pete knows I love animals, and said he had a present for me; a little animal that would light up my life! So when he said "Climb in", I didn't question it! Do you think he is trying to get rid of me? Beware, you never know what's lurking in the bushes!

Today's been one of those days!

All was going to plan, which is unusual in this household! Pete was in Poundbury, looking at a job. I took Steven, after school, to practice his golf; competition on Saturday; Student went 5am this morning! (OK so that was a bit early) Laura at college. Then I realised that Tilley's head collar was half way off and, left alone, could strangle her. So, all hands to the deck (Pete was apparently on his way!) Laura and I were trying desperately to funnel Tilley to the smaller

field then we could get her into the shelter and remove the head collar. What a game. After a while of running like a loony, I realised Mr & Mrs Faddy (Derek and Jan, who Tom accosted last night; he tried to keep Derek in his field for the night! I did warn them that Tom thinks everything on 2 legs is fair game!) were in fact watching us; we must have looked so stupid out there. Then I heard a laugh, and it was Pete up there yapping whilst we were trying to sort Tilley. Eventually,

we managed to get Tilley in the other field, while Pete was still planning it! All sorted, and Bob's your uncle; job done. Now 7.15pm, time for tea! Oh and homework, oh and debrief of Poundbury meeting, oh and let the pigs out, oh and the confirmations that I haven't done yet, oh and the post etc etc. The night is young; we know how to live!

Wednesday 26 September 2007

Time goes so quick ...

Do you know, I have just looked at the calendar and it is October on Monday; that's only 2 clear months until Christmas. OMG. The time has just flown by; I do try to keep you up to date, but I would never leave the computer if I told you everything that was happening here. Sometimes, I wake up and really don't know which month it is, let alone what day it is! Still, it's good for you; well if I believe that, then all will be fine!

Wood all dry for Winter!

I had spent a day moving all the wood in preparation for Pete to stack it in the log shed. He hasn't had time to do this, of course; or was it the inclination? Anyway, it hasn't been done. So, the rain was forecast for the night; told Pete, and he said he would cover it over to protect it and keep it dry. After all, it is our fuel for the winter! I didn't see it when he did it, but when I went out the next morning this is what I saw! here is nothing left to say really is there! So, piece of advice: *never* let an architect cover your wood!

Penelope wants to move in!

Our Peahen Penelope wants to move in, I think. She waits patiently all day outside our guest's doors, waiting for the odd morsel or two. I have invited her in several times, but she can't live inside! I am not sure what will happen in the winter when it gets cold. I am not sure she would like it caged in, so I guess we will continue to let her find her own bed each night. We'll see ...

Strange cloud

I saw a perfect corkscrew cloud from the field. It was huge, and so perfect. The light made it look even better as it caught parts of it, emphasizing the shape. Ran up to get the camera, and this was all that was left of the cloud, but it gives some idea. I have never seen anything like it before; quite bizarre.

Lucky, that's all I need to say!

Today hasn't been easy. Sky is recovering from an operation, so needs to be kept in. Jeff came today and helped us remove the Ivy and paint the conservatory skirtings. So, Lucky had to be limited to the back area, so she wouldn't roll in the paint. We were busy; it must have been all of half an hour, and I thought I better see how Lucky was, as she doesn't like being on her own tooo long! She had Gem, but that doesn't count in her eyes! Well I couldn't believe what I saw; she had actually dug a hole inside the back door in concrete! Now that takes some doing, let alone in half an hour. She is the most expensive piece of nightmare I have ever had in my entire life. What am I going to do with her? Then I ask her what she has done, and she crawls under the table as if she is frightened to death. It just makes me feel really guilty; she's got it sussed I think!

Thursday 27 September 2007

The history of Woodmill explained

We had a great piece of luck the other day; Bill and Sylvia Richardson who used to own Woodmill between 1980ish and 2000 made contact with us after reading this very blog! How mad is that? We were extremely excited about them showing an interest, as they used to keep goats, and won several prizes for them. This is an area we would like to get into; they had their own milk from them, and so on. I need to find out a lot more before we enter the goat keeping world, but its a start! When they lived here, the mill (cottages 1-4) was the goat house, and the laundry another place for either chickens, pigs, or whatever; they had geese in the end of the white stable, and a great dairy in the car park. The pictures they showed us were great; so different to now. They did, in fact, gain the permission to convert to holiday cottages, but never did it. We learned about previous owners, and a history of the Mill. One story involved a pet monkey that used to be in the mill when it was a wood mill after they milled flour. The time flew by; so wonderful to fill some of the gaps. I think they will come back; well, hopefully! and perhaps we can stay in contact. You never know, they may want a holiday!

Tuesday 2 October 2007

Paint, carpets and Pete ... hmm

Well, we have been trying to slot in the rewire of the cottage and a refurb (which isn't going very quickly). So, finally got the ceiling up in the lounge, which was a technical nightmare, but finally up; all we had to do was paint it. I painted the emulsion, and took great care not to spill or drip or splash any paint over anything. Pete then did the egg shell on the beams. It was Farrow and Ball paint and really runny; it dripped everywhere. Pete said "oh, don't worry, we need to replace the carpet", so carried on. Well, by the time we finished, it looked like a Dalmatian! Waited for the log burner to be put in position and done up, and by this time funds were running out; the cat had to have an operation etc etc. Then we realised there was no money for a new carpet. So last night, we spent all night on our hands and knees with scissors, cutting the white paint out of a burgundy carpet! We know how to have fun; although at one point Pete did suggest we just get burgundy paint and paint the white bits to match the carpet!

Pete to the rescue—not

We are so busy with the architectural practice that time seems to run out on a daily basis. And with some major projects on at the moment, ever minute counts. Well, we had a few schedules that needed to go ASAP, and a cottage to change over; I thought I would type up the schedules while I set Pete to work on the cottage. Well, you have never seen anything like it in your life. I couldn't stop laughing; he was in a right pickle when I went down to see him. The bed looked like a teenager had just got out of it, and it was supposed to be ready; he had taken the sofa apart and couldn't figure out how to put it back together, and the hoover had sucked the curtain up. By the time I got down there, he was having a crisis. Think he's better off in the office!

Sky up to no good ... again

Sky is being a real pain at the moment. She is definitely learning from Lucky. She steals toilet rolls and unravels them around the house. She had to have an operation on her leg and have it all stitched up, as a result of which she has to be kept inside for a while, and its driving her crackers. This photo was taken just after she fell out of the curtain; there are claw marks all down the curtain. Nightmare cat. She has also smashed a pottery sculpture by swinging on the curtain pole, a pottery jug that has been with me for 25 years or more, stolen the tassels off the curtains, hidden my glasses, scratched the sofa and pinched the chicken! Not bad eh?

Date

Logs in for the winter

After Pete's attempt to cover the logs up, we decided that they needed to be inside as soon as possible. Pete and Steven work all day doing it. Steven decided to see how many ways he was able to break wood for kindling! But can safely say the wood is now stacked for winter. We have enough for a couple of years I think ...

Ah, Lucky!

Today, Lucky and Gem went on an adventure. No idea where, but they went belting off somewhere, and they knew where they were going, and no one was going to stop them. They finally returned home, absolutely filthy, covered in orange dirt. Lucky was wet also; they looked dreadful. Lucky was obviously the worst, and had to be bathed immediately. She was kind of trying to be good after that and brought me my boot, although she wouldn't let it go. How can you be cross with her with eyes like those?

Found a badger!

We knew there was a badger around here, as we see it cross the field each evening, but didn't realise it had found its way so close to the house. The badger was in with the chickens. I think we came just in time to put the chickens to bed. We shut the hen houses up quickly and ushered him or her out; they have been known to kill 13 or 14 in one night; lucky escape for our Henrietta and billy and Co!

Monday 8 October 2007

A walk in the woods

It's great to be able to access the woods from your back garden, and what a magnificent sight! A break in the trees lets the light fall spectacularly, perfect, except just after this shot. Lucky came bombing behind me, took me out, and I landed in a crumpled heap on the floor, with Lucky returning to see if I was ok; trying to make me better with a soggy slimy tongue! Mmm, nice! *not!*

Where have the cows gone?

Every day I walk the dogs, the cows are in the top field; they are only young, and not sure what breed they are, but great characters. A bit like cartoons really; floppy ears and big noses. I go up to pat them in the morning; they are not sure what to make of me! But then who does? Thought I would share a photo or 2 with you, and this is what I got. The

camera came out, I pointed it at the cow, it ran of, and you've got a gate post, barbed wire and a tree, but there were cows ... honest!

Hay order for Tom!

Tom is growing up; he's on the hard stuff now. Thought I would introduce him to hay, like a big boy! He really didn't know what to do with it; he hit the hay net from side to side with his nose, tried to bite a piece off, and got

the netting. He was in a right pickle, until I showed him how to do it. The things you have to do to keep Tom going. Auntie Sue, where are you now eh? Allright bottle feeding aren't you? Let's see the hay demonstration!

Tom mastered it!

Well, Tom thought he was a cool guy! Yep, finally realised what a hay net was for, got that sussed! He's getting a bit too big for his boots though; as he was hand reared, he doesn't understand to respect humans really he thinks they are a food source. We are gradually getting there though. I was on the ground picking up something, and he jumped on my back; all I could see were his front hooves over my shoulders; it's cute now, but 200kgs later may not be quite so cute so I have to stop him now! He's doing well though ...

Friday 12 October 2007

Mushrooms

Well, not having so much luck really in the identifying of the fungi! But every one we find, we can't seem to find it in our book, so it's either a new species or we are being dim! This photo was taken by the rabbit; quite unusual, a bit like a fairy mushroom! We have found some field mushrooms, although after eating them, we did find a warning in the book which said they can be mistaken for the poisonous one! Didn't feel too well after that!

Woodmill in October

I can't believe our luck at the moment with the weather; it's October but wonderful weather; let's hope it lasts. It looks so idyllic at the moment with the autumn sun. The plants have gone mad here; no sooner do we think we are actually catching up, they all start again. Just cut the Ivy down on the front of the house; it looked nice, but was causing us

real grief with the granite and joints, not to mention the roof and gutters, so I am going to buy a climbing red rose to help the front of the cottage a bit. I know it used to have one there, years ago, so will reinstate it. There is just so much to do, I don't know whether I am coming or going some days ...

Pigs—who'd 'ave 'em?

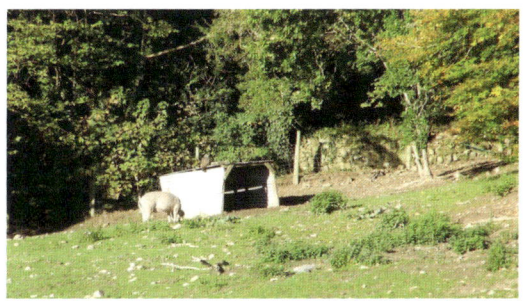

Pete and Steven were at golf—surprise surprise! Steven would live on the course if he could! Laura was busy composing for her A level coursework. And I, in my wisdom, decided to go and see Rosie and Daisy! Well they wanted to come out, so I thought: I bet they are fed up with those kids, and they need a break; Let them out, everything was fine and dandy! Until I went to get them back in; they trotted off, good as gold, down to their home; I opened the gate, Rosie went in, then Daisy stopped; she wanted a cuddle! Just at that point, all 4 piglets went racing out of the gate, and they weren't coming back! To cut a very long nightmare story short, I got them all in one area so when the piglets dug, it was in an area that didn't matter. I rang Laura to come down to help me get them back in. She would only come down if the big ones weren't there; cheers Laura, some help you are! So I was stuck with 6 pigs trapped; no way of moving 6 pigs and it was only 2.30, and the piglets were taking the mick, digging holes that you wouldn't believe, and so quick! What if my guests came? What if Pete's late? what if, what if. Finally, it got to 4.15 and I was still there. I thought I would try to get them back all in one tribe! Finally, with a few hitches, got them back and into bed! What a nightmare; nearly 2 hours wasted faffing about with those darn pigs! I just noticed, in this picture there is a buzzard on the pig shelter! How cool is that?

The bridge to Prideaux!

The bridge is working out just dandy now. We walk the dogs up there every morning; the final steps haven't been built, but it's perfectly fine if you don't mind a bit of a scramble! I still haven't seen those elusive horseshoe bats; one of the only places you can see them is here, but I haven't been lucky enough to see one yet; mind you, I am not the stillest of people, or the quietest, so that probably doesn't help!

Monday 15 October 2007

Just a regular day at Woodmill!

Do you know what? I feel like I am in cuckoo land really, and someone is going to jump out in a minute and say: "Hi, only kidding". First thing, went to Bailey's to get some staples to fix the chicken wire to the steps; looked at the boxes, and asked David how this double ended staple worked, as it was in a "S" shape with points on each end; thought that was pretty nifty, perhaps for turning corners, but how would you use it? I was very puzzled until I saw David nearly on the floor in hysterics! The "S" wasn't the shape of the staple, it was a trade logo for the make of Staples; the staples are in fact, as I found out, "u" shaped! Drove back feeling pretty dim, only to find the dogs had gone on another adventure, the cat had another toilet roll, Pete was busier than ever, the door and telephone were going mad, the cottages needed changing over, Steven needed to be collected from golf, ponies just didn't want to be separated back to their fields, so was running around like a loony trying to sort this; time running out; pigs escaped to top paddock, dogs returned black, pigs finally sorted, ponies eventually sorted, guests arrived. Belinda, one of our guests, came armed with a huge bucket of apples, which was really kind; kids tea! and then I was called to another cottage to hacksaw off someone's lock of their case, as they couldn't get into it. Regular day, really ...

Friday 19 October 2007

Steven has a new bed!

Steven is only 11 and a very important 1/2. That makes all the difference, that 1/2! He has always wanted a double bed, but I said the floor space is valuable, and he would be better off with a single, until today; we got one in the sale, and you would think Christmas had come early twice—the smile on his face was huge. He chose his bedding, and is now extremely comfortable in his very large double bed!

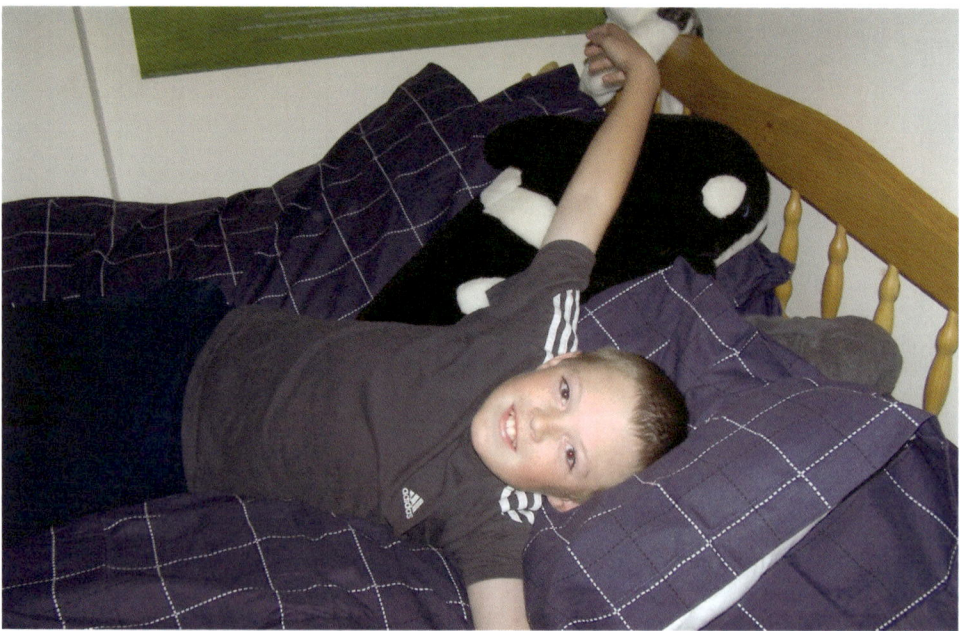

Daisy is nearly a Mum!

Daisy is feeling rather uncomfortable at the moment. She has a belly full of what we hope is piglets, or we have problems! Working on my dates, she should give birth 24th or 25th October. But I am not sure if you count from the beginning of her returning, or end? So it could be as early as this weekend! Watch this space; by the looks of Daisy, she will be glad when its over.

Piglets are getting big now

We still have 4 piglets left; they must be about 4 months old now. The foot and mouth outbreak has hit everyone really hard. Whereas we would have been able to advertise and sell them as weaners, we have to keep them to sell as large pigs now, as soon as the restrictions are completely lifted! They are right little monsters now, into everything! Here's two of them having a mud bath; they play in here for ages, they really have fun. I never realised how much character a pig has until now.

Time for a brew!

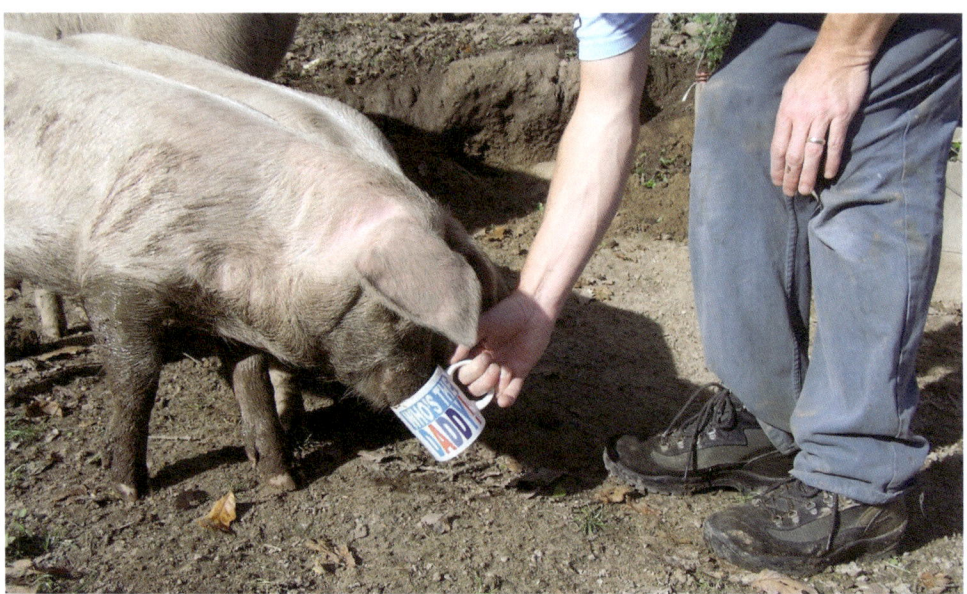

Those piglets will fight for a cup of tea; they like it out of a cup though. After they finished this cup, they were pestering us for more. We have now opened the top paddock for the pigs; it needs clearing anyway. I just hope they don't get out; I'll probably go up in a minute and they will be having a go on the trampoline or something!

Thursday 25 October 2007

Logs

I just thought I would share with you this wonderful coloured piece of wood! So there you go, here it is. I just love it!

Sunrise ...

As we are always up and out before the sun, we have seen some really amazing sunrises so far this year. I took a picture of this one and it looks like St Blazey is on fire! So powerful; it's amazing how much you miss when you are in bed! So come on, get up and see what's going on out there before the sun gets up! Sometimes it's difficult doing the feeds in the dark, but I guess we will get used to it! The clocks go back soon, so that will help.

Steve and Faron

There is definitely something wrong here. I am feeding the animals, whilst Steven and his friend Faron make themselves nice and comfy to play the PlayStation golf or something; they even put a blanket over them to keep warm.

Now that's bad; Lord and Lord muck, cushions for their weary heads! Woodmill, the retirement home for 11 year olds. Mmm, I think not! I know, I know, I am just jealous of such a relaxed pair. Wait till tomorrow; I'll get them working!

Scone maker extraordinaire is 64 today!

Mum, alias nanny, alias chief scone maker had a birthday today—64! I booked tickets to see Kneehigh Theatre, and made a picnic, all set out in individual party bags; salmon, prawns and a whole bunch of party food to take with us. I phoned to confirm the tickets and they told me that there was no food allowed this time. Aaahh, but I had a picnic; well, waste not want not, so we had it before the theatre in the conservatory. Well things just don't go to plan in this house. And if I knew in July when I bought the tickets it was the world rugby cup, I wouldn't have booked them. I got grief from all of them! They enjoyed the play though. So Happy Birthday, Mum!

The tree was pruned

Well, you remember that beautiful Apple tree that I showed you with Steven climbing it? This is all that is left after a pruning session. And it wasn't my fault this time! Jeff came around to prune the apple tree; on closer inspection, a large amount of it was dead, so to save it, we had to take it right back to the main trunk, where hopefully it will sprout from next year; fingers crossed, anyway. I am planning on doing some sculpting with the pieces that were cut off. Mmm, like I am the one with all the time in the world!

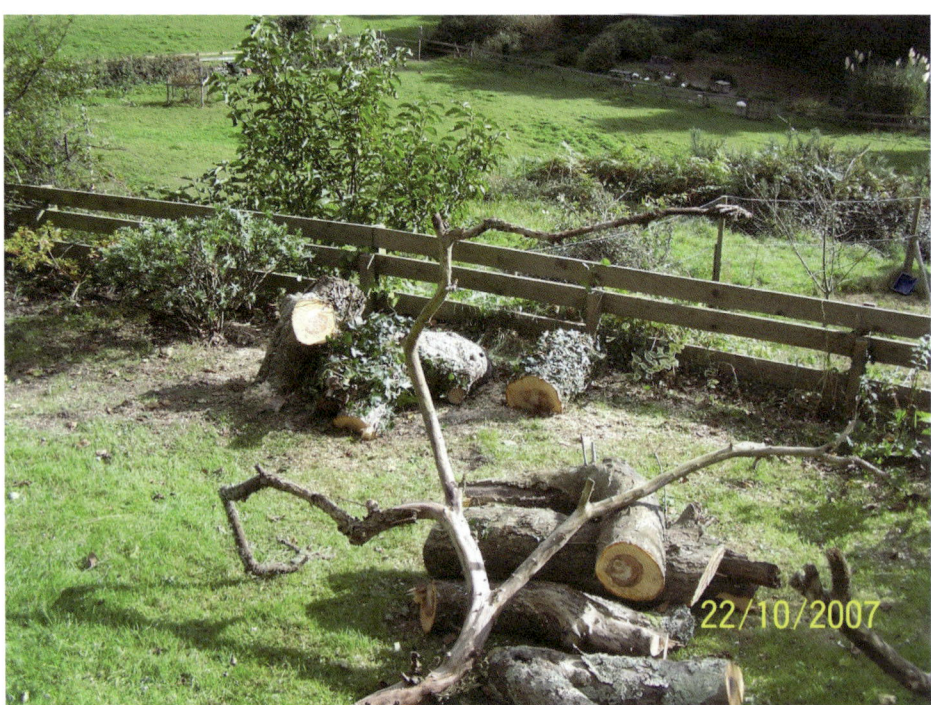

Happy as a pig in muck

The piglets have been let out in the top paddock; it was as tall as me in weeds, but they soon made short work of that! Munching their way through, grunting with happiness! The funniest one was sitting on his backside like a child and just chewing a nut; he was so chilled out and content. They ate themselves to sleep, completely worn out after their busy day.

Sunny arrives

A visit to the RSPCA centre resulted in a phone call to see if I would take a cat. Sunny is a 5 year old fluffy, cuddly, tabby and no one wanted her; she is the most loving cat I have ever met. She only arrived today, but already comes for cuddles; she's great. The new addition to Woodmill. She will be introduced slowly to all the other animals; so far she has got as far as the study and lounge!

Well done Steven!

Wow, great — *well done!* Only 11, and Steven has been selected to represent Cornwall in the Under 14 golf. What a huge achievement. We are so proud of him. He practices every day, and is totally committed, even giving up his football and cricket to give 150%. So, well done. I hope he goes from strength to strength; who knows, a pro may be in the making; Mmm, now where's that car I liked? Only kidding—well done Steven X

Saturday 27 October 2007

Mmm, could have got £250 for that!

Digger driver Mark Richards came today to dig a French Drain in front of the pony shelter; this may help when the rain comes! We just need a concrete slab now inside. To get the digger through the fence, we had to cut the wire. So I jumped up through the flower beds and managed to find the wire cutters. Then ran back to give them to Mark! That's when it went pear shaped; I slipped on the sleeper, fell half way down the flower bed, managed to fall up to my feet in a kind of fashion, then tripped over the wall and fell into the garden of Buttercup Cottage. Not bad eh? Cut hand, elbow and side of thigh. Oh well, all in a day's work, I guess!

The piglets have arrived

29/10/2007

After days of waiting up for Daisy to give birth, the piglets finally arrived early hours on Friday morning! All 10 of them, pink little bodies; they looked so cold. Eventually, they found the heat lamp and snuggled up under it. Daisy isn't such a good mum as Rosie. She isn't so careful; not sure how many will survive! They will have to have their wits about them. Daisy didn't feed them all straight away; 4 were feeding, but the others had to be shown what to do. I put them on Daisy's belly, and they finally had their first feed.

Sunny is settling in nicely!

Sunny is such a loving cat, why anyone didn't want her I will never know. She is so friendly. She met the dogs last night. She didn't run away; the dogs slept, and she sat about 3 feet away and watched them, so that's a start. I think she likes it here. We will keep her in part of the house and gradually let her have more freedom. Mind you, she did come up to the bedroom this morning!

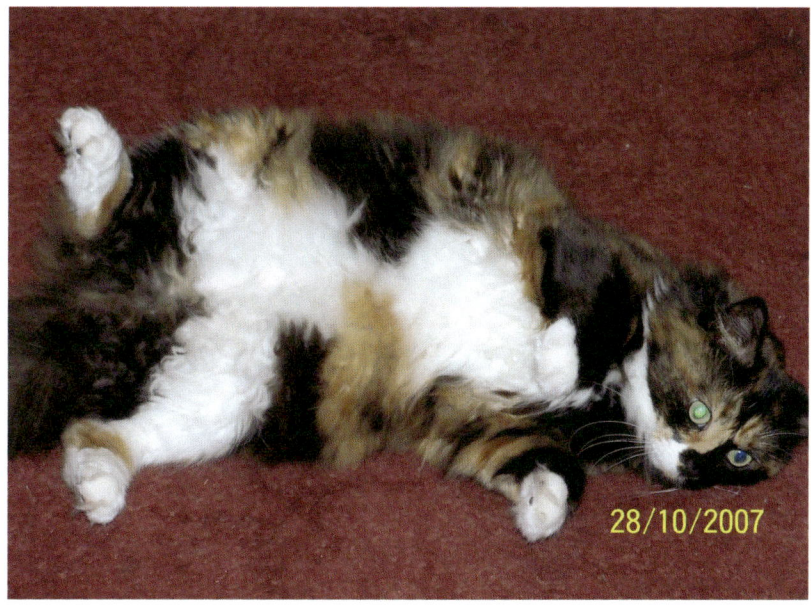

28/10/2007

Tom meets the Farrier!

Tom is 6 months old now and the farrier was due to return! Tom had to have his first trim, and how smart is he now! He was playing the farrier up, but as soon as I cuddled him and he gave me a big sloppy green gooey kiss, he was ok then; he is a right character—he kept looking at the farrier as if to say: "I am only being good cos my mum is cuddling me, so don't get any ideas pal!". His face speaks a thousand words, he's so funny. Duke was better this time; we fed him with vast amounts of pony nuts; not the best for him but hey, it was our health or his belly; his belly won. Marble, Tilley and Storm were all ok; not really chilled, but manageable. So that's 1-1. Let's see what happens in Jan! Watch this space ...

Sunday 4 November 2007

Halloween at Woodmill

Halloween seems to come around real fast these days! Pumpkins scraped out and ready with scary faces; the pumpkin, that is, not us. The children went to mum's house which was decorated in true nanny style for Halloween; apple bobbing, marshmallows on string; the whole caboodle! I think Pete was quite relieved really as last year nanny was away, so we had our party at home. Laura and Steven thought it would be funny to dress Pete up as a manic monster white bunny! He went along with it; he looked real bad, in fact we were afraid to take him out around the neighbourhood! So, year off Pete, make the most of it! (I promised not to put that picture on here!)

Dad's wall

This wall is the handywork of my dad; he missed his vocation in life—dry stone walling is what he needed to do! Not sure he would agree with that. But it looks great; this is only a section of the wall; it was falling down, so he took it apart and rebuilt it, bit by bit. Great, I love it! Cheers Dad! Hope you haven't got too many blisters!

Piglets!

Well, these are what the piglets will look like in about 4-5 months. These are Rosie's litter, well whats left of them; some have been sold. They are right little bruisers! Up to no good all the time—they have discovered that if they throw earth on the electric wire, it doesn't work properly, so they set about doing this and then bust out into the paddock where they can cause absolute mayhem! They are like mini destroyers, uprooting everything as they go; they are funny though— these two posed for the camera!

Sunny, happy as Larry

Sunny is such a happy little cat; not sure who Larry is tho! Anyway, thought I would introduce her to Sky; well that went well—*not!* I brought in little Sky, set her on the floor, and Sunny the chilled, soft, cuddly cat skidded across the coffee table and pinned her to the back of the sofa! I parted them quickly, and all was well, so will have to rethink that process! Mind you, Sky can be a real temperamental nightmare; she rolls and loves the attention, then out of nowhere she will give you a wallop. Maybe Sunny sensed this, and stopped the nonsense before it started; who knows?

Field shelter complete

After waiting for what seems an eternity, we managed to organise the concrete for the base of the field shelter. After waiting for 2 1/2 hours for it to come, we finally laid it before dark! But Tom, dear little Tom, decided he wasn't going to let us do that; he ran over, bent down to get under the gate, and stuck his head in the concrete. I spent the next hour washing his teeth and gums out not to mention his furry beard to stop it from going into a conical hard structure and sticking his teeth together! I couldn't believe he did that; he came from nowhere, he knew exactly what he wanted to do, and did it! That's my boy!

All dressed up ...

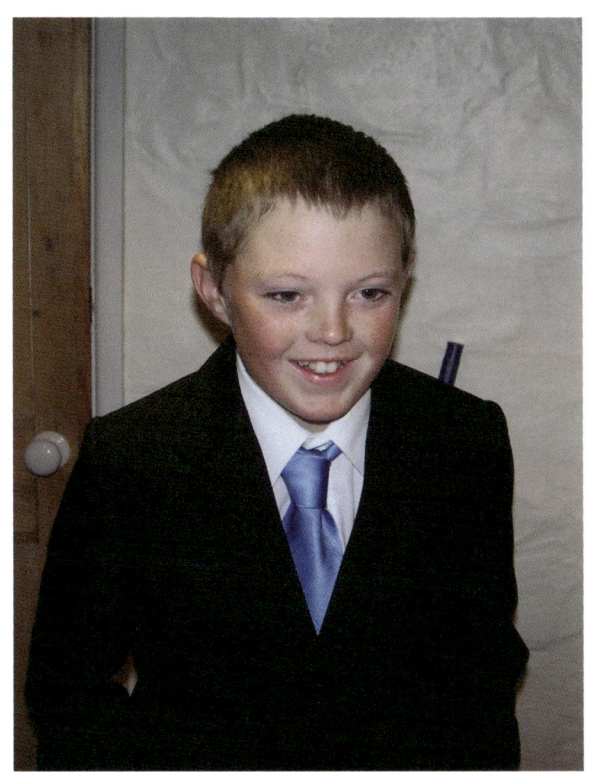

Steven has got the look now; what a bit of a crisis that was—thought it was all going too smoothly! Steven, as you remember from the blog, plays for Cornwall under 14s in golf. Well, he has been playing golf all half term, this competition and that, and a few fun ones too. This particular match was for charity so dropped him off; had the work load sorted for the day, and being Friday it was a hectic schedule! Then Sam, the captain, spoke: "I assume you have all brought blazers with you for the presentation?" DUN DUN DUUUUUNNNN—blazers, what blazer?. Haven't got one, only one from a previous club, which he certainly couldn't wear there! I rang all the major shops (wont mention them as they were all useless and don't deserve a plug!) and no-one had a child's blazer, not anywhere is Cornwall. Time was running out, I now had 1 3/4 hours to sort it! Then a brain wave—rang the mum of the captain and asked her to look if Sam had any blazers he had grown out of, and YES YES YES—we had it in the bag, blazer, shoes the lot; off we went to meet Steven. We were as cool as a cucumber; he'll never know! Just a cool thankyou mum and took it in his stride that this blazer had just appeared as if by magic. Do you know what? I hope he has kids one day!

I can't hear you!

See, even the ducks play that one. I think the one on the right is giving her a right old ear bashing, but she's got the gist, and uses the ol' "I can't hear you" routine! Way to go girl!

Penelope is on a sit-in

Penelope won't move from outside the study door, until I give in and give her some cake; she does this all the time. If I open the door, she comes in; really weird—I keep thinking she will eventually return to her owners, but hasn't done yet. Perhaps when it gets colder, she will fly off to pastures new.

I caught Pete smoking!

Couldn't believe my eyes: Pete, smoking! Well, only kidding. Great piece of wood though, isn't it? It is hollow, and was burning for a long time but it never burnt through; just a hole in the centre filled with smoke; really odd. It's a dead giant flower from the Scillies. Can't remember the name now …

How cute

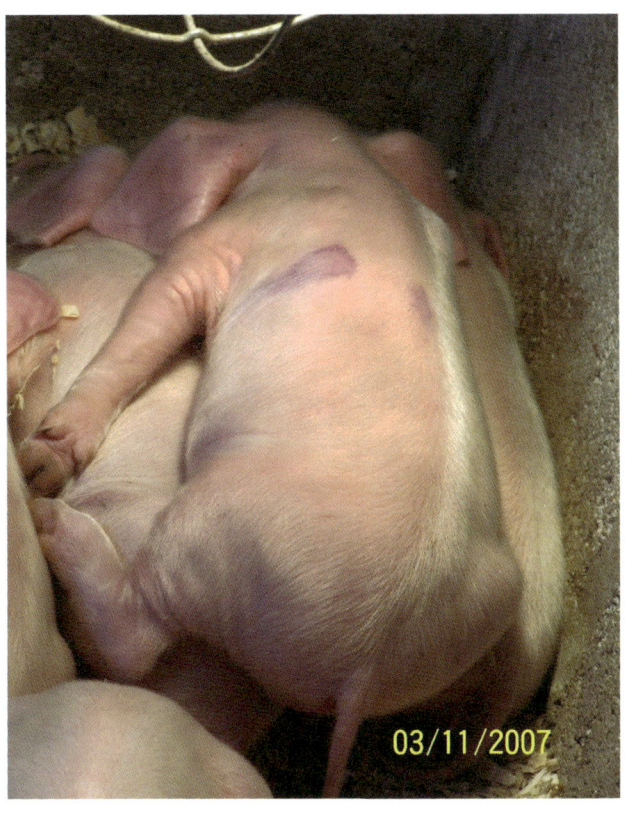

03/11/2007

Daisy's new litter are so adorable; this little one was having a real cuddle with his family, after a belly full of milk. They are a lot different to Rosie's litter, calmer and not so greedy; strange—maybe it's something to do with the birth. Rosie's was fairly traumatic, and Daisy was a bit more chilled about the whole thing; could be ?

Lucky and Steven

Not sure who leads who astray in this partnership. Lucky seems to think everything is a game, and Steven just eggs her on. Both seem to come back from their travels in one piece though, so that's good eh? I think, when I mention I have work that I need help with, they suddenly find something to do!

Built a fire pit!

Pete and I built a huge fire pit, so we could have a bonfire whenever we wanted, and a granite seat to sit on and watch the flames! The only trouble is, Pete lit the fire, but it was all the stuff that me and the kids were saving for bonfire night! All I was able to do was sit and watch our hard work go up in smoke! So, November the 5th came early at Woodmill. We will just have to build another bonfire for tomorrow now!

Piglets

The piglets are just so cute, I must have dozens of pictures of them; all the pictures are different to the trained eye! But all the same to everyone else. It's a bit like showing your holiday snaps to someone: "Here's Billy with a hat on" "Oh and here he is again with it to one side"; how lovely is that? So you see, I am turning into a pig bore! Pardon the pun!

Does it get any better than this?

Steven and I were moving all the chippings to the field shelter to cover the concrete to make it warmer for the ponies to sleep in; I got to ride on the chippings with Gem and Lucky, whilst Steven drove the thing at great speed, trying to bump us all off along the way. Laughing his head off as he put his foot down, all the way down the drive, me screaming all the way down! Dear child! Mind you, by the end of it, we had it sussed on the back; we were surfing the turf! World championships, here we come! Mmm, new sport, I believe!

Tuesday 13 November 2007

Aahh, getting more behind!

It just seems that time goes so quick. Christmas is approaching, and am I ready? Am I heck. Still really busy with the cottages, which is great; architecture side, we are run off our feet, head, arms! And animals, well they just think it's a great laugh to make your life that much more difficult, especially when they know you have not got the time to spare! Steven busy with Cornwall Golf. Laura busy with A-levels etc., and I don't think I will ever catch that elusive tail! Thank goodness for wine!

November the fifth!

November the 5th was here, and nothing was going to stop our bonfire from happening; never had one, and I was darn sure I was gonna have one this year—might be my only chance! Food bought, BBQ to the ready, bonfire built. Set a time when Laura and Steven got home to light it. That's where it went a bit wrong. It was 6.30pm when we all got home. Set up by the bonfire, and it was the blackest night we have had in ages. We had the floodlight torch so we could see! Only Peter didn't put it on charge! So we had T lights and matches, 3 to be precise. The above photo shows how much of a nightmare it was to light the fire; well to be honest, to even find the fire was a challenge, let alone light it!

Got it going tho ...

05/11/2007

Well, never give up; that motto has achieved great things, and maybe some not so good! But we'll forget those! Finally got it lit; the bonfire was ablaze, and we could, sort of, see what on earth we had been eating! Not the most successful night, but the kids won't forget it! Ah, that's what memories are made of! The animals weren't too bad with the fireworks. I was surprised really. We checked the ponies regularly. Obviously we didn't have fireworks, but I mean the ones going off at other places.

Gem is trying to hide!

Gem had to go to the vets this week, she has a skin infection; she is on 2 weeks of antibiotics. She goes through all sorts of undergrowth, so it's no wonder she is poorly. She was trying to hide behind Laura, as she has to have a bath in special ointment; poor Gem; she'll be better soon …

Carpet gone

You remember me telling you about the carpet we stayed up for hours, cutting the bits of white paint out because we found out after we had painted and decided to get a new one that we, in fact, couldn't afford it? Well, you know, that one; well it's gone. I couldn't take it anymore; we still can't afford a new good carpet, or wood on the floor, so we have bought a cheap sea grass thingummybob, and I think we will lay it tomorrow; it's a pig to lay, but I think it will look just fine and dandy for Xmas now; talking of which, 44 days (ish) now!

Penelope has a boyfriend!

Dun Dun Dun—Percy has arrived. Not sure where from, but he flew in, and has taken a fancy to our Penelope. Or did Penelope bring him here? We will never know. But he is here, and looking good. Pete wanted to call him Tarquin at first: "Tarquin the peacock"—hasn't got a ring to it has it? Mind you, I am not that enamoured with Percy, but it's growing on me …

Lulu goes for it!

Lulu is a right character (our *rabbit*; come on, keep up!). She has made a 4ft hole in the front garden; she's going to escape and get eaten, if we are not careful. I need to get a new hutch for her, and then let her out when I can see her. You see, at the mo they have the use of the two runs, all night and all day, as their bed part hasn't got windows; they love it, "they" being Trixie the guinea pig and Lulu. But it's just getting out of hand. Double Decker home. Mmm, I will look for one tomorrow!

Peacocks in love

Ah, how cute is that? Penelope and Percy are in Love, and are due to be wed any day now! They are together all the time at present. Not sure if they will keep together, but I have a hat!

Sunny

Sunny isn't the new kid on the block any more since Percy arrived, and I am not sure what she makes of that; she is keeping a close eye on the proceedings from our bedroom window. She follows Laura around like a lost soul, and likes to sleep with company. Her and Sassy are OK, but Sky is still a bit hissy with her. Sunny isn't phased though; she just sits there with a "doesn't bother me" face!

Pigs and kids

Pigs and kids have a lot in common I think. They are both always hungry, they both always want something, and when you get them both together, something is sure to go wrong. Was trying to do the feed run. Laura was at a music rehearsal; dropped Steven to Cornwall golf, popped back to do the feeds. Got the pig nuts, 6 buckets in fact; fed Rosie, after a battle of wills—I wouldn't let the bucket go, and she wanted it in the wrong area. Fed the big piglets, who are a real nightmare, they are always hungry! Then tried to let Daisy in with one arm, whilst holding Rosie back with one leg, trying not to squish the little piglets with the other arm; argghh! Daisy got to the bucket and fed, so I thought I had cracked it. Then the piglets tried to feed from her, standing; she wobbled a bit, so I jumped in and wedged myself between the wall and Daisy, to stop her from lying on the piglets; then my phone rang. I had to answer it. It was Laura, and she would need to talk to me. So, I tried to answer the phone, dropped it in the feed bucket; couldn't reach it because I was stuck behind Daisy; finally squashed between her front legs and found out what Laura wanted, whilst ushering the piglets to a safe position, and getting Daisy sorted. And that was just the start of the feed run! I had a whole load of others to do yet. Just a regular day in toy town!

Friday 23 November 2007

Lulu and Trixie have a new pad!

Following the 4 foot hole in the front garden, I had to invest in a double-decker rabbit home for Trixie and Lulu. I feel bad about keeping them caged, but it's only at night, for their own safety, and for the good of the garden! They have a new rabbit run, doctored by dad to make it unburrowable, if that's a word. So, by day they can run in and out to their hearts content, and at night they are in their double-decker home. I have even made curtains for them, to keep the wind out; that way, they can enjoy the whole of the run, even if it is raining. I want to come back as my rabbit or guinea pig—what a life they have!

Saturday 24 November 2007

Percy is feeling at home ...

Percy is really taking the mick now. I found him just wandering around in the conservatory. I mean—the cheek of it! The next time I come in, he will be having a party, him and Penelope, with their friends. He wasn't in a rush to go back out.

Sunny

Sunny is settling in so well, it's really strange. She was outside sunbathing a few days ago. She doesn't wander far though, and hasn't really got the hang of the cat flap, but just likes to be around you most of the time. She's just lovely; lets hope Sky doesn't ruin it and teach her any bad habits!

Percy has found his feathers

I am not sure how old Percy is, and whether the tail feathers of a Peacock grow with age, or whether he has them trimmed regularly at the Peacock feather dressers. It's ok, I am kidding; I am not that bad! Mmm, some beg to differ ... well anyway, Percy showed us his tail feathers properly for the first time; ok so he was trying to impress Lulu and did the mating dance for her, but we all get it wrong sometimes don't we?

I shrunk Pete's fave jumper!

I had a little accident with Pete's 100% new wool cosy jumper that he really liked. I put it in the machine on a cool wash, and then forgot it was in there, so when the machine broke with the clothes inside, I re set i and tried to spin the water out, but forgot the jumper was in it. And when I opened the machine, the tiny (extra large) jumper fell out! OH MY GOD! It was so small, it didn't even fit Steven. I hadn't shrunk it to a rectifiable size, I had *really* shrunk it. Steven was in stitches. What was Pete going to say? He came back from his meeting and you know what kids are like; he couldn't wait to say something! Pete's face was a picture …

I was really sorry!

I tried to keep a straight face as Pete tried to get in his tiny jumper. I was saying the right things, but my face wasn't saying the right things. I thought it was so funny. The more he tried to get in the jumper, the funnier it was!

Piglets' first few days out

The piglets are now 4 weeks and haven't been out on their own long. But today was so funny! I let them out with their mum, Daisy, but 4 of them were still asleep. So before I went back up to the house, I thought I better get them all together with their mum. Well, they are so tiny, but they move so quick, and the more I tried to usher them together, the more they moved in all different directions, and I didn't want to lose any. Finally, after an hour of shepherding, I managed it. But I had been running about in the mud for an hour and I looked like I had been mud wrestling! Ah, we live and learn!

The first kiss

Ah, I think Percy and Penelope are falling in love. I caught them kissing yesterday; I wonder if I will need that hat?

Percy is trying his luck!

Percy has got the hang of it now I think; he has finally stopped practicing his mating techniques on Lulu, and moved on to try to impress Penelope! Mind you, he doesn't seem to mind an audience, what with Lulu, Trixie and Sky as onlookers! Not sure what Penelope makes of all that; she is hiding behind the tree! Babies here we come?

Piglets out in the mud

Once the piglets had sussed out the great outdoors, they loved it! They were playing and jumping in the mud, having a great time. Only one couldn't last long without a crafty drink of mums milk! He's going to be a right little porker (pardon the pun). It was lovely to see them. At this rate I won't get anything done, just sit and watch the piglets!

Ponies in the top paddock

The winter is drawing closer by the day, and the grass is starting to slow down. Both the two normal paddocks are looking a little sparse on the grass front. So I rigged up an electric tape to be able to let them into the top paddock. They had a lovely time; what a treat. It wasn't really that well thought out, I must admit. Before I got it sussed with the tape, I did let them up there, but they ran straight up the hill towards the garden and camellias, which are poisonous to ponies. I nearly had a heart attack! But you wouldn't have known that; I was all in control, and just moved my ponies to the top paddock!

Lucky

Lucky just can't help herself; if she's not up to no good, she's meddling with someone's bed. She kicked the cat out of her basket and stole the basket; put it by the Rayburn, and tried to go to sleep in it. It's about 5 sizes too small, but that's Lucky for you!

Tuesday 27 November 2007

We have a famous poet!

A little rest and relaxation for our poet to write some fine masterpieces! If you haven't heard of her then you must look at her work—Jo Bell. She has a great website: www.bell-jar.co.uk. You can see some of her work, and contact her about workshops, which we are hoping to offer here at some point; needs thinking through though. I can't believe she read my blog; aaargh, all these grammatical errors, to put it mildly, and madness. Oh well, maybe it inspired her in some way! Great person, great positive energy; thanks for coming, Jo.

Sunday 2 December 2007

"I'm too sexy for the frost" says Duke

Duke: what a man! He's out there strutting his stuff, posing for the camera and the girls, who are all hiding in the shelter opposite. Tilley, Marble and Storm and little Tom are all huddled up in the field shelter. Not Duke; he's a real man (so he thinks!) ...

Wine tasting!

We had a great night with a couple of our guests, learning from the masters (Mr & Mrs Packham) on German wine. It was so kind of them to invite us down for the evening. We tasted quite a few. Do you ever go in a supermarket or restaurant and pooh pooh German wine? Well, I know I have a few times. But this was exquisite. Mr & Mrs Packham venture over to parts of Germany and, as Chris can speak fluent German, it would be a little easier for him than me, and bring back vast amounts of wonderful wine. You see, apparently, in the supermarkets, we only get a blend of wines, and not the true German wine. The wine we tasted was so pure and tasty; no chemicals, just fermented grapes. I am certainly hooked. I have put it to them that we perhaps organise a wine tasting event at Woodmill and sell the goodies. I am sure it would be a sell-out. I learned a great deal that night, thanks to Mr & Mrs Packham!

Still frosty!

It has been a bit nippy the last few days, but so pretty. The mornings are white and crispy, and the animals look so good in it! Mind you, I did threaten to give them all a hot chocolate in case they were feeling the cold. You can see all the ponies following Pete in hope of the hot drink. Pete's warm jacket has come in handy (I am in the warm taking this photo from the bedroom window!—I'm not silly!).

It's nearly Christmas!

I love Christmas. The sooner it comes the better. Just love it! We started in bits and bobs as Pete's not quite as keen as us on the whole thing, especially in November. So started with a little tree in the lounge; thought we would break him in gradually! Laura and Steven decorated it. Just makes you forget any problems, doesn't it? Aahh …

This has got to be a joke!

Found Lucky, quiet as a mouse, not even a peep. She had only gone and kicked out all of Sunny's litter tray and gone to sleep in the tiny plastic tray. *What is wrong with her?* Just because I was busy in the office and wouldn't let her sit in the lounge. You see, they only come in the lounge in the evenings, when they are ready to settle down, and our office is the other side of the lounge, and she wanted to be with us.

But really this has got to be the best yet. Does anyone else have a dog like Lucky? Doubt it!

Sunny is not amused!

Sunny just is not amused with Lucky's antics. Is there nothing sacred around here? Can't a girl have dignity now? Poor Sunny; I just can't believe it.

... and a few more decs ...

Little by little, we are adding bits and pieces to our Christmas decorations. Put the reindeer together (ah, Derek and Jan (Faddy) ... you thought I was kidding when I said I will put the booking through after I have put the reindeer together didn't you? You should have known better!). I think it's looking quite Christmassy now; ready for Santa to come down the chimney!

Storm and Tom on the run

We let Storm and Tom out in the top paddock, and soon realised we should have electrified the tape and not just left it. Storm and Tom, Houdinis of the pony world, were out on an adventure. I caught them coming up the path towards the house. But as soon as they saw me, they realised they shouldn't be up there. Camellias and things were up there. Not the sort of place that is good for a pony! Eventually got them back and rigged up the tape. All safe for the moment. Cute though, aren't they?

And then there were outside lights!

27/11/2007

A few little lights to brighten up the rabbit's world; you can't really see them here, but we have a couple of reindeer and some trees and stars and a few (160!) lanterns in the tree. I am trying to persuade Pete to help me put the lanterns on the top of the guttering, but it's not going well at the mo! Could be me up that ladder tomorrow at this rate! They are not very bright, so they look quite sweet, and I have never had outside lights , so it's another one off my to-do list!

Time to reflect

It's really odd; it is December already, and a year ago today, we were waiting for a move-in date for Woodmill Farm. It's a world away from what we were used to. Pete employed as a director, me with my own business, suits, meals, entertaining; all the fake things that come with corporate life, only it seems real when you are in it. It's only when you get a brief look at the other side of real life you question these things. I won't repeat how we came to be here, as you can read it on the first few entries on this blog. But who'd have guessed Finland would have made such an impact on our life, thoughts and more importantly, our souls. It was instant; we knew straight away our life was going to be very different when we returned from Finland.

Laura ... time out

Laura and Steven had the best time in Finland. Our log cabin was away from anyone else, and had its own jetty and boat; we rowed and fished and BBQd each night, not forgetting the sauna and birch leaves! We lived very simply and trekked to see the Caribou and many other beautiful wild animals, unspoilt by anything—perfect!

Sunset from our log cabin

Sunsets, wine, fresh BBQ fish caught by your own fair hand. No TV, no Radio, just a log cabin, fire, BBQ and us. Why would you need anything else?

Just had to share this with you ...

01/12/2007

Well, you can count on Pete to bring you back from your reminiscing thoughts. I was in another world for a minute. Then Pete shouts in and says "Have you got a pair of pliers, because the heat lamp has fallen out and its raining real hard?" Perfectly OK request, except he thought there was nothing wrong with his attire. Lucky had pinched his boot and it had filled with water in the storms today, so he had to find another one! But instead of putting another pair on, he simply found another boot of some description and thought that was OK. I am so glad it's dark; he's been out walking about the farm like that! Seriously, what am I going to do with him? I can only apologise for those who may witness his antics!

Tuesday 4 December 2007

Toga party!

Well, have you ever seen a toga like these? Laura had a Toga party with Truro College (she is the one on the left as you look at the picture). When I was at school/college, a toga was a sheet that wrapped around you in quite an unflattering way; my how things have changed! These take on togas seem to have a poetic licence! Way to go, Laura!

It started yesterday!

Yesterday my bracelet broke and I put it into Pete's pocket for safe keeping until I got home. Forgot! Put it in the wash! Blocked the washing machine! Meanwhile, Purl design is so busy you wouldn't believe; working through the night! Oscar (boar) arrived back. The pig pen wasn't/isn't ready but hey, who cares? Piglets everywhere. Pete gets washing machine out on the floor. And I mean out, insides 'n all! Man for the blinds came for the holiday cottages, whilst window cleaner trying to do the windows open; unexpected client turned up, had to get a form faxed, not got a fax; good old Walter Bailey came up trumps again (thanks guys), you saved my bacon yet again! Pigs still all over the place, washing machine in bits, Pete in a stress. Lucky then joins in, eats my cheque book, underwear, cat bed, welly! Cat in litter tray, making an almighty stench. Steven needed collecting; he wanted to get a fir tree for the porch, and I gave in as I promised, alledgedly! Laura comes home, can't move her thumb due to an Octave key on the Saxophone. Decorated tree in a wholesome fashion! (not!) Client gone now. Steven feels sick. Pete is shouting for help. Oh I forgot, cut Stevens hair in the middle of all this, and homework, and golf practice. It's now only 8pm and my kitchen looks like a hell hole, and Pete is still taking more bits off the machine; thought I'd share this with you! Good news though; found my bracelet. Bad news: working through the night yet again. Merry Christmas y'all!

Tuesday 11 December 2007

Windy!

It has been a real rough weekend weather wise. The Cornwall Golf was called off; electrician was lucky and used the weather as a genuine excuse. He better hope he comes tomorrow! Trees down all over the place, force 9 gales, rain, hail, wind, and this little munchkin thought it was a good idea to stay in bed; well a lie-in anyway. It was 9am before he got up and, believe you me, that's late in this house! The weather is forecast to calm down a bit next week; let's hope so; we have gutters to clean, pigs to home, arcs to build, shelters to form etc etc ...

Lucky looks very guilty

Not sure what she has been up to, but I called Lucky and Gem in after a little adventure, they both came in extremely sheepishly. I think they may have got in to a spot of bother, and hoping I won't find out! I have, however, found the end of the hose attachment that Lucky has chewed and hid in her bed! Maybe that's it. She jumped on the table and looked very sorry for herself—very strange ...

The table arrived

We have been waiting a while now for our table to be finished, and it was finally ready to collect yesterday. The wood we selected was planks of old Cornish Elm and had a table made from it. It's absolutely stunning. If you want anything made, marquetry or simply stunning bespoke furniture, then contact this guy: Stephen Roberts of Wood Design, near Wadebridge (www.wooddesign-furniture.co.uk). A very talented man! I went out for a mo after admiring our table (I am very excited about the table, can you tell?) and Laura sneaked in with the dogs and her tea! And shabby old sauce on my new bespoke table! Talk about cheek! Is nothing sacred here?

Sunny? ... or Jess?

Sunny has taken to her tea like a duck to water. She rather likes the postman pat cup! Could it be Jess that's of interest to her? (for those not up on these things, Jess is Postman Pat's cat; I know this after years of forced watching postman pat with the children!)

Revising?

Laura, although only in her first year of college, has A-Level exams in January, and should therefore be busy revising, especially Maths! But I think she has flipped; this is how I caught her! Maybe the pressure is getting to her! Good job I only photographed this small bit of her bedroom! You should see the rest. Pieces of paper everywhere with some sort of assumed mathematical theory on it, or bits of half worked on manuscript from music. I am assured it is work in the making! Mmm, not sure; we'll see!

Tuesday 18 December 2007

This is what happens when you keep putting me off!

See, Alan our electrician doesn't really know how important the festive season is to us at Woodmill, I love it! So when I asked that outside power was put in before the 1st of December, and he agreed, I expected it to be done! But Alan kept putting me off, hoping it would go away; you see, if he came when he said he was going to, a month ago, it would have been warm and light, instead of cold and dark! But all in now, albeit a month late! He'll learn!

Shoe homes have arrived!

Nothing is too much of a challenge to my Dad! He's up for just about anything, so when we mentioned shoe houses, suddenly one appeared! Little slates on the top, and painted grey! They are so cute; so now you can put you shoes under cover outside your cottage if you have been out walking. There is also a bike and walker's store but this is in the car park; these handy little houses are right outside your front door. I guess I should copyright it. I guess that's all done now! So if you wish to purchase one of these, I am sure we can come up with a suitable fee! Thanks, Dad; they are great, talent must run in the family! (wishing!)

Trees going up!

After a right fiasco with the electric, and trees sent back, then re-ordered, finally we were putting up the fiber optic Xmas trees. I put them up and they all blew over, so before I threw them across the decking, as I have just about had enough, Pete came to my rescue and screwed them to the deck; all looks pretty and festive, ready for our Christmas guests.

New bowl ... new bed!

Sunny has settled in so well, I bought this bowl from the garden centre, iron ring bowl. Well, Sunny thought it was fair game; she hadn't slept there before; comfy? I think not, but she was going to stay there!

And I thought Christmas was busy before Woodmill!

I am not sure if I am coming or going or went! I have sorted out the feed for the Xmas period now, after running around trying to make sure everything was in stock, list done for mum and dad when they are here after Xmas for the feeds, cottages well on the way, replacing some equipment and ordering lots of furniture and things you wouldn't believe. I had a 4 page list, and certainly haven't finished yet; sourced the paint for the painting in January; bought presents, wrapped 'em! sent to Santa! food on order; god knows if that will come, or in fact it will be the right things? Saturday is Christmas change over. Pete and Steve at golf with Colin and Tim (brothers). Sunday muck out and sort final cooking for the Xmas eve do. Pete at golf comp with Steven (he will have to do his jobs when he gets back!), open house you see ... silly me! usually over 50 people pass through the doors, eating and drinking: no problem! Arrghh; then clean up, prepare Xmas lunch for next day, feed reindeer, Santa, wait for him to arrive, get up at a stupid time to unwrap them! Eat! Boxing day swim for charity! Then off to Switzerland, after a major changeover with mum and dad; hope they will be OK, it's quite busy here; hopefully I will do all possible before I go so that it runs pretty smoothly! So you see, nothing to it really if you say it real quick, and miss out lots! And I wonder why I am seeing double and dizzy? Oh gotta go, see ya; got feeding to do, it's getting dark already ...

Wednesday 26 December 2007

Tights and PVA!

As if I haven't enough to do! Laura was invited to a friends 18th birthday and needed a fairytale outfit. So Laura being Laura left it to the last minute to share this with me, followed by: "I need a fairy outfit for tonight"! We had to clean all the cottages first for the Christmas changeover, but hey, I am up for a challenge; it's amazing how much you can fit in! So PVA, Pair of tights, tinsel, wire, red furniture spray and glitter: Bob's your uncle—wings! Outfit made, wings all ready and kinda fairy here we come!

Ready to party

Laura and Hayley are as bad as each other. Nothing normal about either of them, but great to have around. I think they had quite a few invites to people's parties as they were the ones having a great time on the dance floor; nothing inhibited about these pair!

Mr and Mrs Santa

We always have a bit of a bash on Christmas Eve. I get that excited about Christmas, and unless we do something, I wouldn't be able to cope. So we dress up as reindeers, Santas and Elves and have drink and food until it's time for church at 5.30pm for the Chrisdingle service.

Steven

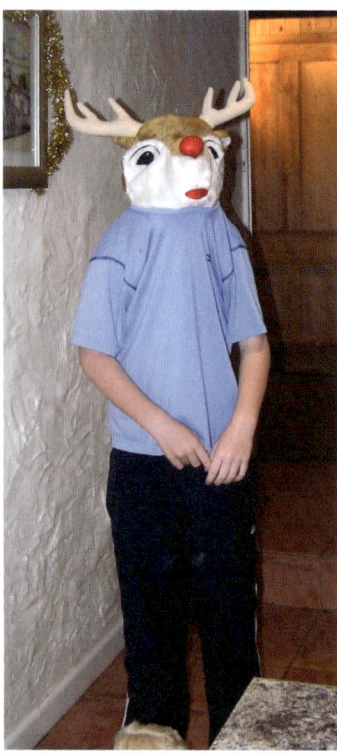

Steven likes to dress up for Christmas eve, but somehow boredom of the itchy outfit takes over very quickly! This is what's left of his reindeer outfit!

Dressing up

Well, Christmas Eve isn't a place to turn up if you haven't got an outfit. I always have spares, and am quite happy for people to borrow them, even if they don't really want to! I try to talk most people into it! They agree in the end! Laura had a few spare antlers! And well, Hayley's up for anything! So, Elf it was!

Fish supper

The famous fish turns up every Christmas Eve. It's kind of traditional now; ham, fish and food; it takes absolutely ages to make this fish, but everyone seems to enjoy it. I may do a duck next year, and see if anyone notices!

Busy!

It's been so busy trying to sort everything out this year, and just as you think you have it sorted, either a radiator packs up, or people arrive late, or you pack everything away and realise you need the thing at the very back of a garage. Santa seems to take it's toll! I think it's all worth it, though. I guess it's what memories are made of!

The Elf and Reindeer

At the end of a long exciting day, and Santa was on his way; the elf and reindeer got attitude! Must have a word with those Santa's little helpers; think they are getting too big for their boots—now, where's that Santa? He'll sort them out.

Early Christmas morning

It was just perfect to see the animals wake up for Christmas day; we had a treat for them all, and I think Tom took a liking to my outfit; he slobbered all up the side; cheers Tom! (if you don't usually read this, Tom is the miniature Shetland pony, in case you are wondering!) Marble, shown above, is Tom's mum, and may be in foal again!

Lucky and the Elf!

Lucky is so funny; she gets so excited. I think she knew it was Christmas. She opened her present and then skidded across the floor, took it to her bed, and you didn't hear a peep out of her for quite some time; think she might like it! We were supposed to meet up with a potential mate for her this Christmas, but time just flew by, and all that went out the window. I will have to look for a man for her after Christmas; I think I have until Feb. Knowing my luck, she will escape and mate with a shiatsu or something!

Santa came to the pigs

Nothing gets left out here; even the pigs got a special little treat from Santa, and served in festive coloured new buckets. I bet not all pigs get this treatment!

Little things!

It doesn't take much to please these two! A wind up boat and a flipping duck (in the true sense of flipping!). They were very happy bunnies; I think the golf trolley and clubs, money for car, clothes and a host of other things may have helped a little? Do you think?

All I want for Christmas is a banana!

That was Laura's wish list, and she got it! A five foot foam banana! She is getting sponsors at the mo for a charity boxing day swim, and guess what? She is going in dressed as a banana. So, not only is she going to freeze, she will look like a giant banana! Sponsors are coming in now, and I think she has raised about £120 so far; this will be split between the pilot gig club (its a boat in case you didn't know and they race all over the place; the world championships, which Laura has been to, is held in the Isles of Scilly; she didn't race this year as she had a hernia; maybe next year) and Churchtown farm, which helps children and young adults with disabilities access activities, so worthwhile doing!

Ducks got a pressy from Santa too

Can't forget the ducks; mind you, they just stood all over my wellies and were more interested in the barley than their treat from Santa. Don't even think they noticed I had dressed up for the occasion!

Aahh Gem

Gem is a star. I am not sure our dogs realise they are dogs; they are either up to no good, or soft as sugar, you just can't imagine the trouble these pair get in when you see them like this. Little angels!

Santa looking for Dinner!

He'll be out of luck in the oven; by the time we have fed the animals, dinner sort of comes as an after thought! We did manage to get a full dinner, with a stupid amount of different vegetables on the plate; lovely Salmon to start, and Xmas pud for desert; but Santa came too early to pinch it; the Rayburn was bare!

Santa's little clan

The ponies looked so cute with Santa, it was like feeding the reindeer on Christmas morning; how lucky are we? Hard work has paid off; it's perfect here. Wonder if I will be thinking that later, when everyone else is sat watching TV and we are out seeing and mucking out the animals?

Mum and Dad to look after farm

We are off to Switzerland soon, skiing, and I wonder how it's going to go back here; mum and dad are going to look after all the animals! So Pete bought me a planner to write messages on before I go. If he thinks I can get all my instructions on this, he's crazy. I have pages of them!

Trixie and Lulu

A little pressy for Trixie and Lulu: a tunnel. Now that we have stopped Lulu digging to Australia, with chicken wire, I felt that she needed a tunnel. They were very grateful. This Christmas lark is an expensive hobby!

What does this face say to you?

Is this the face of gratitude? I think not. We gave mum a tambourine for Christmas, and she loved it; she has always wanted one, and also we thought she may like to bring out the creative side of her, from the murky depths and believe you me, its deep! So we bought her a canvas for her to experiment; not really sure what she made of it — what do you think?

How many cooks!

Well, they all want to get involved in the good bit—where were they all when I was cooking it?. It's dish-up time, and it was all hands on deck for the very large Christmas dinner event!

Vicky? ... I think not

I've been had! I took a booking for Vicky, a daughter of my uncle Chris's partner. So, right until the last minute I was expecting Vicky! Emails flying to and fro, money exchanged hands, all the usual stuff! Then, on the 22nd, larger than life, my aunt from Spain, you know the one, nettle woman!... and Doug ... grass man! were stood in my kitchen, telling me they were in Buttercup cottage. So I said no, you can't, its all cleaned for Vicky, but I have another cottage, or you can stay here. I didn't want them to think they were not welcome. I would find somewhere for them; but she was insistent they were going in cottage 5. It took ages for the penny to drop; that Vicky did not exist; it was, in fact, these pair on the biggest wind up ever! Extremely pleased to see them, though. All I could think of was: I must get more sprouts for xmas dinner!

Tired Lucky

Lucky was so tired; it was her first Christmas, and all she wanted was a cuddle and a sleep—with Santa!

Piglets for the off

Piglets are 8 and a bit weeks old now, and three of them were to be picked up and settle into their new homes. Sarah came with her children, and loved them, they loaded them carefully into a dog carrier, and off they went. Only 7 left now!

The Before picture!

This was Laura, before the cold sea took its toll on the giant banana; will she do it?

She did it!

Well, Laura does my head in sometimes! She told us: no, no, don't have to be there until 11.30 to sign in! Got a phone call to say "Where are you?" from my mum, who was organising the event. We raced across the town, ran down to the beach, and only just registered in time for the swim; what am I going to do with her? She did look good though! A wet soggy banana, but all in a good cause; banana with fishnets too!

Happy New Year!

We are off to Switzerland the day after tomorrow, so just in case I don't have time to log on again, I wish you all a very Happy New Year and I hope it's a really good one for you all; thank you to everyone who made our first year possible; the help from my Mum and Dad, Louise & Doug, Jeff, Paul and Annie who have been there from the start and extremely busy! websites, photos, advertising, help and kind words, great people to work with; thanks for everything. Also, I don't know what I would have done without our Laura, so thank you Laura, we make a formidable team, and thank you to Steven for all that polishing! and of course, thank you to all of you who have visited us and shared your thoughts, life and ideas with us. Happy New Year XX

A RAINBOW

As I sat all forlorn,
My gaze was drawn to a crystal millpond; where the light periodically bounced from the silver skin of the sea – only to be ruptured as it lapped the intrusive line of the cliff edge, retreating, effortlessly, smoothly and peacefully, restoring its completeness and unity.

I watched in awe at the captivating beauty, symbolic of life and pure representation of freedom, the epitome of living.

Then as if from nowhere an arc of radiant light encircled the moment, filled with perfection of colour. Imposing its glory on all that cared to see.

It stood majestic and noble, exquisite yet refined. All these qualities enshrouded within one awesome phenomenon. It stood for a fleeting moment, and in an instant disappeared, leaving me with a feeling of contentment; like somehow it had appeared just for me, at a time my thoughts were with you. It was reminding and reassuring me, that you were just at the other end of that rainbow; that somehow always connected, part of the perfectly formed crescent, so maybe apart in body but never in soul.

By Michelle Hume

My life inspired by Nan (Elizabeth Hannah Harvey) and made complete by Pete (my husband), Laura and Steven (my wonderful children).

xxx

Printed in the United States
1331LVUK00005B